Abraham Elzas

The Book of Job

Translated from the Hebrew text with an introduction and notes, critical and

explanatory

Abraham Elzas

The Book of Job
Translated from the Hebrew text with an introduction and notes, critical and explanatory

ISBN/EAN: 9783337189389

Printed in Europe, USA, Canada, Australia, Japan

Cover: Foto ©Lupo / pixelio.de

More available books at **www.hansebooks.com**

THE BOOK OF JOB,

TRANSLATED FROM THE HEBREW TEXT,

WITH AN INTRODUCTION

AND

NOTES, CRITICAL AND EXPLANATORY,

BY

A. ELZAS,

Translator of the "PROVERBS OF SOLOMON."

LONDON:
TRÜBNER & Co., PATERNOSTER ROW.
TO BE HAD OF
P. VALLENTINE, 34, ALFRED STREET, BEDFORD SQUARE, W.C.,
AND OF THE TRANSLATOR.

1872.

ENTERED AT STATIONERS' HALL.

PREFACE.

Encouraged by the favourable reception which his translation of the Book of Proverbs has received from the press and the public, both Jewish and Christian, the translator now sends forth a new version of the Book of Job.

As was his desire with respect to the Book of Proverbs, so here also he hopes to make the English reader better able to understand the Divine original than he is from the authorised version.

The Book of Job, being far more difficult to translate intelligibly than the Proverbs, he has bestowed much care upon the critical and explanatory notes, and consulted the ablest commentators within his reach.

He begs also to acknowledge his particular obligations to Mr. T. W. Cox, from whom he has again received much assistance in preparing the work for the press.

THE TRANSLATOR.

24, BELGRAVE STREET,
      LEEDS, *January*, 1872.

INTRODUCTION.

The moral of this divine poem must, in all ages, be consolatory and important. A virtuous and good man, suffering the greatest reverses of fortune, and enduring the severest afflictions, is tempted by the harsh judgments of his friends to consider his sufferings as the effect of his sins; or to doubt the justice and mercy of his great Creator. He persists in vindicating his own general character and conduct; and after a long period of disease and affliction, which was intended for his trial, he is restored to greater happiness and prosperity than he had enjoyed before.

The great outlines of Job's history, it is probable, were founded in fact*; the account of the existence of such a man is regarded as historically true by an inspired writer of the Scriptures. In Ezek. ch. xiv., v. 14, we read: "Though these three men, Noah, Daniel, and Job were in it [the land], they should deliver but their own souls by their righteousness, saith the Lord God." Here Job is referred to as *a real character* as distinctly as Noah and Daniel. If then we have no doubt that there were such men as *Noah* and *Daniel*, there is no reason why *Job* should be regarded as a fictitious character, and so far as the historical record goes, there is the same evidence of the actual existence of the one as of the other.

Not all the learning and critical sagacity of past ages have been able to decide, with any probability, *where* Job lived, *when* he lived, *when* the book was written, in *what language* it was written, or by *whom* it was written.

I. THE QUESTION WHERE JOB LIVED.

We are told in the first chapter of the Book, that Job lived "in the land of *Uz*." This land of *Uz*, is probably Idumea, as appears from Lam iv. v. 21. Idumea is a part of Arabia Petraea, situated on the southern extremity of the tribe of Judah; Numb. xxxiv. v. 3; Joshua xv. 1, 21. The land of *Uz* therefore appears to have been between

---

* Samuel bar Nachman believes, that "Job did not exist, and was not a created man, but that the Book of Job is a parable;" Hai Gaon and Rashi alter this passage and say, "Job existed and was created to become a parable;" Rabbi Levi ben Gershon (Ralbag) treats it as a philosophical work; Simcha Arieh denies the historical truth of the narrative, on the ground that it is incredible the patriarchs of the chosen race should be surpassed in goodness by a child of Edom.

Egypt and Philistia, Jer. xxv. 20, where the order of the places seems to have been accurately observed in reviewing the different nations from Egypt to Babylon ; and the same people seem again to be described in exactly the same situation Jer. xlvi.

Eichhorn also supposes that the scene is laid in Idumea, and that the author of the poem shows that he had a particular acquaintance with the history, customs, and productions of Egypt. (Einleitung § 638.) Good supposes that Uz was in Arabia Petraea, on the south-western coast of the Dead Sea, and that Job as well as his friends were Idumeans. (Introductory Dissertation, § 1, pp. vii.—xii.) Gesenius, Rosenmüller, Spanheim, Lee, Umbreit. and Noyes suppose that *Uz* was in the northern part of Arabia Deserta, between Palestine and the Euphrates. Bochart, Michaelis, and Ilgen suppose that Job lived in the valley of Guta, near Damascus.—The Rabbinical writings afford no aid in finding a clue to his place of abode.

Barnes, on the authority of the Rev. Eli Smith states, that there is still a place in the Houran called by the Arabians *Uz*, and that there is a tradition among them, that that was the residence of Job. It is northeast of Bozra, which was once the capital of Idumea, though it was situated without the limits of their natural territory. If this be so, then Job was *not* an Idumean.

II. THE QUESTION WHEN JOB LIVED.

There is as much uncertainty in regard to the time *when* Job lived, as there is in regard to the place *where* he lived.

In the Talmud (Baba Bathra, fol. 14) the Doctors disagree. According to one Job lived in the time of Moses, according to others he lived after the Babylonian captivity.

I would rather accept the opinion of those who suppose that Job lived in the time of Moses, or perhaps in the time of the patriarchs. As reason I would argue, that there is a striking want of allusion to the Jewish rites, manners, customs, religious ceremonies, priesthood, festivals, or fasts. Such allusions we should expect to find, had the Author lived after the exode, and who thus would have been familiar with the customs and religious rites of the Israelites.

The general belief of the Talmudists (see Baba Bathra fol. 14) was that Job belonged to the Abrahamic race ; but even admitting that Job was a child of Edom, and that the Author meant to preserve this impression distinctly, yet his residence could not have been very far from the Hebrew nation ; and one who manifested such decided principles of piety towards God as Job did, could not but have a strong sympathy with that nation, and could not but have referred to their rites in an argument so intimately pertaining to the government of Israel's God. The only reason for *not* alluding to any Jewish rites or ceremonies must thus be found in the fact that he lived *before* the exode, and *anterior* to the institution of the Jewish rites.

III. THE QUESTION WHEN THE BOOK WAS WRITTEN.

I have remarked before, that in the Book of Job there are no allusions to such events as a writer would have made, had he lived *after* the exode. There is no allusion whatever in the Book to Moses; no indisputable reference to the Egyptian bondage, to the departure out of Egypt, to the scene at the Red Sea, to the Manna, or to "Mattan Torah," (the revelation of God's Holy Will on Mount Sinai.) We find no reference in the Book to the Judicial or Ceremonial Law, no mention of the festivals, not a single name of the Jewish Tribes.

Many of these events would have furnished the most apposite illustrations of the points maintained by the different speakers of any which had ever occurred in the history of the world. Nothing could have been more in point on numerous occasions in conducting the argument, than the destruction of Pharaoh, Israel's deliverance, the care evinced for them in the wilderness, etc., etc.

So obvious do these considerations appear, that they seem to settle the question in regard to the time *when* the Book was written, viz., that it was written *before the Exode.*

IV. THE QUESTION WHO WAS THE AUTHOR OF THE BOOK, AND IN WHAT LANGUAGE IT WAS WRITTEN.

The name of the Author is nowhere mentioned, either in the book itself or elsewhere in the Bible; hence it is impossible to arrive at absolute certainty, and it must be a point of mere conjecture.

The Talmud does not mention with certainty the Author; we are indeed told (Baba Bathra, fol. 14) that "Moses *wrote* his book and the book of Job;" but there being a difference of opinion among the Talmudists *when* Job lived, and some of them supposing that he lived after the Babylonian captivity, the latter could consequently not 'hold Moses as the *Author* of the book.

Herder supposes that it was written by some ancient Idumean, probably Job himself, and that it was obtained by David in his conquest over Idumea. He supposes that in the latter writings of David, he finds traces of his having imitated the style of this ancient book (Hebr. Poetry, I., 110). Rosenmüller, Spanheim, Reimer, Stauedlin, and Richter, suppose that it was composed by some Hebrew writer about the time of Solomon. Luther, Grotius and Doederlein hold Solomon for its Author. Umbreit and Noyes believe it was written by some writer about the period of the captivity, Kennicott, Michaelis, Dathe, and Good hold Moses as the Author. Warburton regards it as the production of Ezra. Lowth, Magee and Prof. Lee regard it as the work of Job himself.

By such variety of opinion it is impossible to arrive at absolute certainty.

I have already stated that in my opinion the Book was written anterior to the exode; this would lead us to believe that Moses was the most likely person for the authorship of it. Still several circumstances lead us to the conclusion that Moses was *not* the Author.

The style of the Book is not that of Moses; it has a foreign cast. It differs from the usual style of the Hebrew compositions. The allusions, modes of thoughts, and figures of speech, to one who is familiar with the writing of the Hebrews, have a foreign air. The style of thought and the general cast of the Book are Arabian. There are in the Book an unusual number of words, whose root is only found in the Arabic, and more aid can be derived from the Arabic language in interpreting this book, than in the exposition of any other part of the Bible. (See the commentaries of Schultens and Lee, Castell's Lexicon, and Gesenius' Geschichte der Hebraischen Sprache und Schrift, Seite 33). Aben Ezra says: "In my opinion, the Book is a *translation*; hence we meet with so many difficulties as we usually find in a translated work." *

If we take these circumstances into consideration, we may well come to the conclusion that the Author must have been an Arabian by birth, and that it was originally written in the Arabic language. Job himself might have been the *Author*. He lived 140 years after his trials in prosperity and happiness; he had thus ample time to make the record of his trials. To judge from his speeches, he was well able to compose the Book. He was by far the best speaker of all; and he who was competent in such severe trials to give utterance to the lofty eloquence, the argument, and the poetry now found in his speeches, was certainly not incompetent to make record of them in the long period of health and prosperity which he subsequently enjoyed. These remarks, however, do not forbid us to suppose that, if the Book were composed by Job himself, the last two verses in ch. xlii., containing an account of his age and death, were added by a later hand; as the account of the death of Moses (Deut. xxxiv.) must be supposed not to be the work of Moses himself, but by some later inspired writer.

On the other hand there can be little doubt in holding *Moses* as the *translator* of the Book into Hebrew.

He spent forty years in various parts of Arabia, where, if such a work had been in existence, it would be likely to be known. His talents and training at the Court of Pharaoh were such as would make him likely to look with interest on any literary document; especially on anything having the stamp of uncommon genius. The work was eminently adapted to be useful for his own countrymen, and could be employed to great advantage in the enterprise which he undertook of delivering them from bondage. It inculcated the necessity of submission without murmuring, under the severest trials; and it showed that God was the friend of the righteous, and that, though they were long afflicted, God would ultimately bestow prosperity upon them.

It seems to me, therefore, that the Book was composed by *Job* himself in the period of rest and prosperity which succeeded his trials, and came to the knowledge of *Moses* during his residence in Arabia, and was adopted by him to represent to the Hebrews in their trials, the

---

* Rénan (le livre de Job, Paris, 1859) gives another reason for these difficulties. He says: "Cet antique monument nous est parvenu, j'en suis persuadé, dans un état fort misérable et maculé en plusieurs endroits."

duty of submission to the will of God, and to furnish the assurance that He would yet appear to crown with abundant blessings His own people, however much they might be afflicted.

One great object of this Divine Book seems to have been to establish the uncontrolled Sovereignty of God, and to administer the true consolations of religion, founded on the justice and mercy of God to every human being that is suffering in this world of trials, under any extraordinary visitations of Divine Providence. These great ends will be answered, whether the book was written by Job himself, by Moses, or by Ezra; whether it was originally composed in Hebrew or Arabic; whether it appeared for the comfort and instruction of mankind; while the Israelites were under the iron rod of Egyptian bondage; when they were suffering a state of wretched bondage in Babylon; or when they first returned to their own country and were preparing to rebuild the walls and temple of Jerusalem.

V. THE DIVISION OF THE BOOK.

The Book of Job consists of six parts, viz.: An opening or exordium, containing the introductory history and decree concerning Job;—three distinct series of arguments, in each of which the speakers are regularly allotted their respective turns *;—the summing up of the controversy;—and the close and catastrophe, consisting of the suffering hero's grand and glorious acquittal and restoration to prosperity and happiness. The first part contains the two first chapters. The second extends from the beginning of the *third* to the end of the *fourteenth* chapter. The third begins with the *fifteenth* and concludes with the *twenty-first* chapter. The *fourth* reaches from the *twenty-second* to the close of the *thirty-first* chapter. The *fifth* contains the summing up of the controversy by Elihu, and extends from the *thirty-second* to the end of *thirty-seventh* chapter. The *sixth* part includes the remaining chapters of the Book.

---

* See my remarks Ch. xxv. v. 1.

CHAPTER I.

1. There was a man in the land of Uz, whose name was Job, and that man was perfect and upright, fearing
2. God, and avoiding evil. And to him were born
3. seven sons and three daughters. And his substance was seven thousand sheep, three thousand camels, five hundred yoke of oxen, five hundred she-asses, and a very great estate; so that he was greater
4. than any of the men of the east. And it was a custom with his sons to make a family-feast, every one on his own birthday, and they sent and invited
5. their three sisters to eat and drink with them. And when the days of feasting had gone round, Job sent and sanctified them; and rose early in the morning, and offered up burnt-offerings according to the

---

1.—*The Land of Uz.*—See Introduction.—*Uz* was the grandson of Seir, the Horite. See Gen. xxxvi., v. 20, 21, 28. He inhabited that mountainous tract, which was called by his name antecedent to the time of Abraham; but his posterity being expelled, it was occupied by the Idumeans. See Deut. ii., v. 12.

3.—*Men of the East.*—The men—the children of the East, seems to have been the general appellation for that mingled race of people (as they are called, Jer. xxv., v. 20), who dwelt between Egypt and the Euphrates, bordering upon Judea from the south to the east; the Idumeans, the Amalekites, the Midianites, the Moabites, and the Amorites. See Judges vi., v. 3; Isa. xi., v. 14.

4.—*Birth-day.*—We learn from Herodotus, that it was a usual custom among the Orientals to celebrate *birth-days* with great festivity.

5.—*Sanctified them.*—He prepared them by various lustrations, ablutions, and other ceremonies to offer sacrifice. Compare Exod. xix, v. 10, I Sam. xvi, v. 5, where the same word means to prepare themselves by ablutions to meet God, and to worship Him.—*And renounced God.*—Good contends that the verb "Barach" should be understood in its regular sense, *to bless*; and that the conjunction *vau* should be translated *nor*. "Peradventure my sons may have sinned, *nor* blessed God in their hearts."—Boothroyd: "It may be that my sons have sinned *though* they have blessed God, &c." He follows Noldius.—The A. V.: "and *cursed* God in their hearts." I

number of them all, for, said Job: "It may be "that my sons have sinned, and renounced God "in their hearts." Thus did Job continually.——

6. Now on a certain day, when the sons of God came to present themselves before the Lord, Satan also came
7. among them. And the Lord said to Satan: "Whence comest thou?" Then Satan answered the Lord, and said: "From going to and fro in "the land, and from walking up and down in it."
8. And the Lord said to Satan: "Hast thou considered "my servant Job? For there is none like him on "the earth, a perfect and upright man, fearing God
9. "and avoiding evil." Then Satan answered the Lord, and said: "Doth Job fear God for nought?
10. "Hast not Thou made a hedge about him, and "about his house, and about all that he hath on "every side? Thou hast blessed the work of his "hands, and his substance is increased in the land.
11. "But stretch forth Thy hand now, and destroy all "that he hath, he will then, indeed, renounce Thee
12. "to thy face." And the Lord said to Satan: "Behold, all that he hath is in thy power; only "against himself stretch not forth thy hand." Then Satan departed from the presence of the Lord.——

reject these translations on the following grounds :—There are in the Heb. language *verbs* and *nouns* indubitably homogeneous and expressive alike of both affirmation and negation. Such *verbs* we meet with very often; the meaning in the "Piel" being the very contrast of the meaning in the "Kal." Now the stemword "Berech," in its normal signification, means *the knee*, and the verb "Barach" *to bless*, expresses the act of adoration, the bending of the knee.—The negation of such service is a renouncement, a witholding. In this sense, and in this sense only, we can render the verb "Barach" in its negative meaning.—Job was afraid that his sons might have for the moment abandoned or renounced their religious duties.

6.—The Targum: "And there was a day of judgment, in the "beginning of the year, and the troops of Angels came, that they might "stand in judgment before the Lord."—See I Kings, ch. xxii., v. 19-22.

7.—*Going to and fro.*—The Targum: "I am come from going round "the earth to examine the works of the children of men." The expression *going, walking*, means in the Heb. idiom vigilant execution of any office. See Zech. 1., 10, 11.

12.— The Targum: "Departed *with authority* from the presence."—

13. And on a certain day, when his sons and daughters were eating, and drinking wine in the house of
14. their eldest brother; A messenger came to Job, and said: "The oxen were ploughing, and the
15. "she-asses were feeding beside them; And the "Sabeans fell upon them, and took them away; "and the young men they have smitten with the "edge of the sword; and I only am escaped to tell "thee."——
16. While he was yet speaking, another also came, and said: "The fire of God fell from heaven, and hath "burned up the sheep, and the young men, and "consumed them; and I only am escaped to tell "thee."——
17. While he was yet speaking, another also came, and said: "The Chaldeans appointed three bands, and "rushed upon the camels, and carried them away, "and the young men they have smitten with the "edge of the sword; and I only am escaped to tell "thee."——
18. While he was yet speaking, another also came, and said: "Thy sons and daughters were eating, and "drinking wine in the house of their eldest brother;
19. "And behold, a vehement wind came across the "desert, and smote the four corners of the house, "and it fell upon the young people, and they "are dead, and I only am escaped to tell "thee."——

13.—The Targum: "The first day of the week."—

14.—*Sabeans.*—If it could be ascertained, that there were inhabitants of that part of Arabia, which is called *Sheba*, it would serve materially to fix the part of the country in which the scene of this dramatic poem is laid. From the Bible we know that Jokshan—son of Abraham by Keturah—begat Sheba. Gen. ch. xxv., v. 3. The Targum: "Lilith, queen of Zamargad, rushed suddenly upon them."

16.—*Fire of God.*—Most probably *lightning*, as *thunder* is called *the voice of God.*

17.—*The Chaldeans.*—They were descendants of Nahor's son "Chesed." hence *Chasdim* or Chaldeans.—These people, addicted to rapine, must thus have made their predatory excursions from the borders of the Euphrates to the borders of Egypt.—

20. Then Job arose, and rent his mantle, and shaved his head, and fell to the ground, and worshipped,
21. And said:
"Naked came I out of my mother's womb,
"And naked shall I return there.
"The Lord gave, and the Lord hath taken away ;
"Blessed be the name of the Lord."
22. In all this Job sinned not, nor did he ascribe indiscretion to God."

CHAPTER II.

1. Again on a certain day, when the sons of God came to present themselves before the Lord, Satan also came among them to present himself before the Lord.
2. And the Lord said to Satan: "Whence comest "thou?" And Satan answered the Lord: "From "going to and fro in the land, and from walking
3. "up and down in it." And the Lord said to Satan: "Hast thou considered my servant Job? "For there is none like him on the earth, a "perfect and upright man, fearing God, and "avoiding evil ; and still he holdeth fast his "integrity, although thou didst move me against
4. "him to destroy him without cause." And Satan answered the Lord, and said : "Skin for skin, yea, "all that a man hath, will he give for his life.

20.—*Shaved his head.*—It was a usual sign of mourning among the Jews and neighbouring nations, to shave the head.—In Jerem. ch. xli., v. 5., we read that four score men lamented the desolation of Jerusalem, having their beards shaven, and their clothes rent.

21.—*And naked shall I return there.*—The Targum adds : "To the house of burial," Dr. Good remarks, that the origin of all things from the earth introduced, at a very early period of the world, the superstitious worship of the earth, under the title of Dameter, or the *Mother Goddess*—a Chaldee term probably common in Jdumea at the time of the existence of Job himself.

1.—*Again on a certain day.*—According to the Targum it was a year after the former trial.

3.— *Destroy him.*—Houbigant: "That I might trouble him in vain."

4.—*Skin for Skin.*—The Targum: "*Limb* for *Limb*," i.e., a man will give anything to save his life, yea, he will rather part with his *limbs*, if only his *life* can be spared.

5. "But stretch forth Thy hand now, and touch his "bone and his flesh, he will then, indeed, renounce
6. "Thee to Thy face."—And the Lord said to Satan: "Behold, he is in thy power; only spare his "life."——
7. So Satan departed from the presence of the Lord, and smote Job with ulcerous sores, from the sole of his foot to the crown of his head.——
8. Then he took a potsherd to scrape himself, and he
9. sat down among the ashes. And his wife said to him: "Dost thou still retain thine integrity?
10. "Renounce God and die."—But he said to her: "Thou speakest as one of the impious women "speaketh. What? Shall we receive good from "God, and shall we not receive evil?" In all this Job did not sin with his lips.——

7.— *Ulcerous sores.*—This disease is supposed to be the *Judham*, or black leprosy of the Arabs.—It was named *elephantiasis* by the Greeks, from its rendering the skin like that of the Elephant's, scabrous and dark-coloured, and furrowed all over with tubercles.

8.—*To scrape himself.*—To remove the ichor that exuded from him, and to ease the intolerable itching which attended his disease.—*Among the ashes.*—Persons under extreme sufferings appear to have considered *ashes* as affording them an asylum, or as the means of deep humiliation and atonement.

9.—The Targum: "And *Dinah* his wife said unto him." The Sept.: "Much time having elapsed, his wife said unto him: "How long dost thou stand steadfast saying, behold I will wait yet a little while looking for the hope of my recovery! Behold, the memorial of thee has disappeared from the earth—those sons and daughters, the pangs and sorrows of my womb, for whom I toiled laboriously in vain. Even thou sittest among loathsome worms, passing the night in the open air, whilst I, a wanderer and drudge, from place to place, and from house to house, watch the sun till his going down, that I may rest from the toils and sorrows that now oppress me. But speak some words towards the Lord, and die." Whence this addition had its origin, it is impossible to say. No doubt it was written by some one as a paraphrase in the margin of a Bible, and inserted in the text by a transcriber.—*Thine Integrity.*—By "*integrity*" we are to understand here that soundness of principle, which led Job to repose the most perfect and unshaken confidence in the justice and goodness of God.

10.—See Ch. i., v. 5.—The Targum: "Thou speakest like one of those women who have wrought folly in the house of their father."— *Impious.* Or Atheist. See Ps. xiv., v. 1.

11. Now three of Job's friends heard of all this calamity which was come upon him, and they came every one from his own place; Eliphaz the Temanite; Bildad the Shuhite; and Zophar the Naamathite; for they had agreed together to come to mourn with him and to comfort
12. him; And when they lifted up their eyes afar off, and knew him not, they raised their voice and wept, and they rent every one his mantle, and sprinkled
13. dust on their heads toward heaven. And they sat down with him on the ground for seven days and seven nights, and none spake a word to him; for they saw that his grief was very great.——

PART 2
CHAPTER III.

1. At length Job opened his mouth, and cursed the day of his birth.
2. And Job exclaimed and said:
3. Perish the day wherein I was born,
And the night it was said: "A male is conceived."

11.—The Targum: "And the three friends of Job heard of all the calamity which had come upon him, and when they saw that the trees of the gardens were dried up, and that the bread of their meals was turned into living (raw?) flesh, and that their drinking wine was turned into blood, they came each from his own place, and for the merit of this they were freed from the place destined to them in Gehenna."

13.—*None spake a word.*—They thought that he was suffering for his sins; and in his present deplorable state, would not aggravate his misery by reproaches.

2.—*Exclaimed.*—So RASHI.

3.—*Perish the day.*—A similar expression of feeling is made by Jeremiah. See ch. xx., v. 14–16. The Targum: "Perish the day in which I was born, and the angel who presided over my conception."—*It was said.*—Gesenius: "Which said." Sept: "In which they said." Good: "The night which shouted." Reiske proposes to read "immi" *my mother*, instead of "amar" *said*, thus: "And the night in which *my mother* conceived a male." This reading would be supported by Jerem. xx. v. 14.—*A male is conceived.*—Sept.: "Lo! a male!" They read "hinneh" *lo*, instead of "harah" *conceived.*—In fact it is difficult to understand how the night of conception could be known. Tacitus (Annals xiv., 12) mentions that the Roman Senate, for the purpose of flattering Nero, decreed that the birthday of Agrippina should be regarded as an accursed day.

4. That day—let it be darkness,
   Let not God from above inquire after it,
   Neither let the light shine upon it;
5. Let darkness and death-shade claim it;
   Let a cloud dwell upon it;
   Let day-darkness make it terrible!
6. That night—let a gloom seize it;
   Let it not rejoice with the days of the year;
   Let it not come in the number of the months!
7. Lo! let that night be solitary;
   Let no joyful voice come therein!
8. Let them curse it who curse the day;
   Who are ready to rouse the crocodile!
9. Let the stars of its twilight be darkened;
   Let it long for light, and there be none;
   Neither let it see the eyelids of the morning!

4.—*Inquire after it.*—So Herder. Job wished that even God should forget that day, and take no notice of the doings on that day.

5.—*Claim it.*—Let darkness resume the dominion over the day, and exclude the light.—*Day-darkness.*—Herder: "Let the blackness of misfortune terrify it." Good: "The blasts of noontide." Sept.; "Let the day be cursed." The Targum adds: "A day similar to that in which Jeremiah was distressed for the destruction of the house of the Sanctuary, or like that in which Jonah was cast into the sea of Tarshish."

6.—*Rejoice.*—Nearly all the versions consider this verb as "yachad," *to join, to unite.* I consider it as "chada," *to rejoice.* This is in accordance with the masoretic points, and this sense of the verb is highly poetical.

7.—*Let no joyful voice come therein.*—The Targum: "Let not the crowing of the cock be heard in it."

8.—*Who curse the day.*—Those who hate daylight, as murderers, thieves, adulterers.—*To rouse the crocodile.*—This expression may be proverbial for persons who are in such a state of despair, as to be tempted to rush on certain destruction. Nearly all the commentators on this verse vary. Homberg translates: "Let them curse it who curse their birthday, those who are ready to deplore their cohabitation." Rashi nearly the same.

9.—*Twilight.*—"Neshef" denotes both the *morning* and *evening* twilight, but here it is the latter. Job wished that the evening of that night should not be illuminated by stars.—*Eyelids of the morning.*—"Shachar" means the Aurora, the morning.

10. Because it closed not the doors of the womb to me,
    So as to hide sorrow from mine eyes! ——
11. Why did I not die from the womb?
    Expire when I was born?
12. Why did the knees anticipate me?
    And why the breasts that I should suck?
13. For now had I lain down, and been quiet;
    I had slept; then had I been at rest
14. With kings and councillors of the earth,
    Who build desolate places for themselves
15. Or with princes that had gold,
    Who filled their houses with silver;
16. Or why was I not as an hidden abortion?
    As infants which never saw the light?
17. There the wicked cease from troubling;
    And there the weary are at rest;

10.—*Because it closed not the womb to me.*—According to Aben Ezra, *God* is meant here. But why not *day* and *night*, who are here personified as having been active in bringing him into the world? According to the Targum, Job is speaking of the *umbilical cord*, by which the *foetus* is nourished in the womb. Had this been shut up, there must have been *an abortion.*—The affix to "Beten" must be understood in a passive sense.

11.—*From the womb.*—Why was I not *still-born.*—*When I was born.* (Literally: "When I came out of the belly.") Why did I not die *soon after* my birth.—Sept.: "Why did I not die *in* the womb."

12. *Anticipate.*—This is the true meaning of the verb "kadam," and refers to the tender affection of the parents to anticipate the wants of a new-born child.—Dr. Gill would read: "Why did the knees *receive* me," and observes that it may be understood of the father, who usually took the child upon his knees as soon as it was born. Hence the goddess Levana had her name, causing the father in this way to own the child.

14.—*Desolate places.*—Good: "Who restored to themselves the ruined wastes." I believe it means *mausoleums*, which kings constructed, where they might lie in solemn grandeur.

15.—*Houses.*—Sepulchres, mausoleums, in which it was customary to deposit much of the treasure which the dead possessed when living.—We are informed by Josephus, that great treasures were buried in the tomb with David, which were afterwards taken out for the supply of an army. See Schultens *in loco.*

16. The proper place of this verse, is after verse 12.—*As infants.*—Miscarried before the time of birth.

17.—*There.*—In the *grave*, not in *heaven* as some suppose.

18. There the prisoners rest together;
    They hear not the task-master's voice;
19. The small and the great are there equal;
    And the servant is free from his master.——
20. Why is light given to him that is in misery,
    And life to those bitter in spirit?
21. Who long for death but it cometh not;
    And dig for it more than for hidden treasures;
22. Who rejoice at the tomb;
    Who exult when they find a grave?
23. To the man whose way is hidden,
    And whom God hath hedged around? ——
24. For my sighing cometh before my food,
    And like water are my cries poured out.
25. Verily what I feared hath befallen me,
    And what I dreaded hath come upon me!

18.—*Rest together.*—Herder: "There the prisoners rejoice in their freedom." Sept.: "There they of old assembled together have not heard the voice of their exactor." A most curious rendering.—*Task-master.*—The account of the treatment of the slaves in Mesquinez, is a lively comment on this passage. Their task-masters deliver them over at night, as so many sheep, to another, who has charge of them all. This man secures them in one house till next morning, and then they hear the doleful echo of "Come out to work."

19.—*Free.*—Professor Wolfsohn: "Many a servant more free than his master."

20.—Schultens remarks that the tone of Job's complaint here is considerably modified.

21.—*Who long for death.*—Who would regard it as a privilege to die.

22.—*At the tomb.*—I have followed Professor Wolfsohn. This reading is confirmed by a Hebrew MS. of Kennicott, which reads "gal" instead of "gil." Houbigant also accepts this various reading, which yields an apposite and suitable sense.

23.—*To the man.*—Why is light given to the man whose way is hidden.

24.—*Before my food.*—Preventing him from taking his daily nourishment.—So Rosenmüller. Good: "Behold, my sighing takes the place of my daily food." Schultens: "My sighing comes in the manner of my food." *Like water.*—His groans and complaints resembled the murmuring sound of distant waterfalls.

25.—When Job heard of *one* calamity he naturally expected and feared *another* would follow. So Good, Gill, Schultens, and Rosenmüller.

26. I had no peace; I had no quiet;
Yea, I had no rest as the trouble came on!

CHAPTER IV.

1. Then Eliphaz, the Temanite, answered and said:
2. If we attempt a word with thee, wilt thou take it ill?
But who can refrain from speaking!
3. Lo! Thou hast instructed many,
And the weak hands thou hast strengthened;
4. Thy words have upheld the stumbling,
And the feeble knees thou hast established.
5. But now it has come upon thee, and thou faintest;
It toucheth thee, and thou art troubled.
6. Is thy piety then nothing?—thy hope!
Thy confidence?—or, the honesty of thy ways?

26.—The Vulg. and Targum read this verse interrogatively: "Was I not in safety? Had I no rest? Was I not in comfort?—Yet trouble came."

1.—*Eliphaz.*—Eliphaz was the son of Esau, and Teman was the son of Eliphaz. Gen. xxxvi., v. 10, 11. This Eliphaz was no doubt of this race. Teman, a city of Idumea: Jer. xlix., v. 7, 20; Ezek. xxv., v. 13; Amos i., v. 11, 12; Oba., v. 8, 9.

2.—Eliphaz knew that he was about to make observations which might implicate Job, therefore he introduces his remarks in the kindest manner.

3.—*Instructed many.*—How to bear their trials, and thou hast encouraged the desponding.

5.—*But now.*—It is thy turn to suffer. *And thou faintest.*—Thou makest no use of the principles which thou didst recommend to others.

6.—Eliphaz says, that he should put his trust in God still, and not reproach Him. I have followed Schultens and Professor Wolfsohn.—Nearly all the commentators on this verse vary. Houbigant: "Was not thy religion thy confidence; thy hope, the integrity of thy morals?" Dr. Waterland: "Is this thy reverence, thy confidence, thy hope, and the integrity of thy ways?" Rosenmüller: "Is not in thy piety and integrity of life, thy confidence and hope?" The Vulg.: "Where is thy fear, thy fortitude, thy patience, and the integrity of thy ways?" The Sept.: "Is not thy fear founded on folly, and thy hope and the evil of thy way?" Noyes: "Is not thy fear of God thy hope, and the uprightness of thy ways thy confidence?" Heath: "Is not thy fear, thy folly, thy hope, the integrity of thy way?"

7. Remember, I pray, who ever perished being innocent?
   Or where were the righteous cut off?
8. As I have seen, they who plough iniquity,
   And sow mischief, reap the same.
9. By the blast of God they perish;
   And by the breath of His nostrils they are consumed.
10. The roar of the lion, and the voice of the fierce lion,
    And the teeth of the young lions are disappointed;
11. The old lion perisheth for lack of prey,
    And the whelps of the lioness are scattered.———
12. Unto me an oracle was secretly communicated,
    And mine ear caught a whisper thereof,
13. In thoughts from the visions of the night,
    When deep sleep falleth on men,
14. Fear came upon me, and trembling,
    Which caused all my bones to shake;
15. Then a spirit glided along before my face,
    The hair of my flesh stood on end;

7.—*Remember.*—Eliphaz suspected that Job would not have been subjected to such calamities, had he been so pious as he had professed to be.

8.—*Reap the same.*—The fruits thereof. See Prov. xxii., v. 8; Hosea viii., v. 7.

9.—*By the breath.*—By his anger.

10.—Five various names are here quoted by Eliphaz for the lion. The Arabs boast that they have four hundred names by which to designate the lion.—*Are disappointed.*—The passive of the root "Ta'ah." This suits the connection better. The A. V. considers it as the passive of the root "Latha."

12.—Eliphaz professes to have received a vision from God. Perhaps he did so to give more authority to the doctrine which he was now stating to Job.—*Caught a whisper.*—The Hebrew word "Shemetz," according to Gesenius, means a transient sound rapidly uttered, and swiftly passing away. According to Castell, it means a sound such as one receives when a man is speaking in a hurried manner, and when he cannot catch all that is said. This is no doubt the idea here.

13.—"It is in vain to search through ancient or modern poetry for a description that has any pretensions to rival that upon which we are now entering." GOOD.—Virgil has attempted such a description (Aen. II. 772), but it is far inferior to this of the Sage of Teman.

14.—*Fear.*—The Targum: "A Tempest."

16. It stood—but it's form I could not discern;
    A figure was before mine eyes;
    There was silence, and I heard a voice—:
17. " Shall mortal man be more just than God?
    " Shall man be more pure than his Maker?
18. " Lo! in His servants He putteth no trust,
    " And His angels He chargeth with frailty;
19. " How much more those who dwell in houses of clay,
    " Whose foundation is in the dust,
    " Who are crushed before the moth-worm!
20. " From morning to evening they are cut down,
    " Unregarded they are ever perishing.
21. " Doth not their very excellence pass away?
    " They die, even without wisdom."

16.—*A voice.*—Grotius supposes that it was the *Bath-Kol*, "daughter of the voice," mentioned by the Talmudists—the still and gentle voice in which God spoke to men.

17.—*Mortal man.*—Rather *feeble* man.—*Shall man.* "Geber," a *strong, mighty* man. Good, Noyes, Boothroyd, Rosenmüller and others have a different translation: "Shall mortal man be just *before* God? Shall man be pure *before* his Maker?" They allege that it could not have been made a question whether man was *more* pure or just than God. But I believe that my translation, which is supported by Rashi and the Targum, will fully do justice to the original. Job, who had charged God with injustice, and who had seemed to be wiser than God, is reproved by Eliphaz, who says: "Can *man* then be *more* pure and just than the Almighty?"

18.—*Servants.*—The Targum: "In his servants, the prophets, he does not confide."—*Frailty.*—Nearly all the translators vary on the meaning of the word "Tehalah." Gesenius and Kimchi, from "halal" *to be foolish.* Good: *default.* The Vulgate: "In his angels he found *perverseness.*" French translation: "He *puts light* into His angels." Syr. and Arab.: "And He hath put *amazement* in His angels." Coverdale: "And *proude disobedience* amonge His angels." The idea is that even the holiness of angels cannot be compared with God.

19.—*Much more.*—The particle "Af" has the sense of *addition.*—*Foundation*—Rashi: *grave.*—*Moth-worm.*—See Calmet; also Niebuhr's "Reisebeschreibung von Arabien," Seite 133. Rashi: "Consumed by worms."

20.—*From morning.*—In almost every moment some human being departs from this world.—*Unregarded.*—The event being so common, it is little noticed. How true this sentiment!

21.—*They die.*—Before having had time to become wise. The Targum, interrogatively: "And shall they not die without wisdom?"

V. 1. Call now! Is there any one who will answer thee?
And to which of the Holy Ones wilt thou appeal?
2. Truly wrath killeth the fool,
And indignation slayeth the simple.
3. I have seen the fool taking root;
But I marked his abode for sudden destruction;
4. Far from safety are his children;
They are crushed in the gate,
And there is no deliverer;
5. His harvest the famished devoureth,
And seizeth it to the very thorns;
And the thirsty swallow up their wealth.
6. Truly affliction cometh not forth from the dust,
Nor doth trouble spring out of the ground;

1.—*Is there any one.*—Noyes: "See if He will answer thee?" *i. e.* see if God will enter into a judicial controversy with thee. Good: "Which of these will answer for thee?" He supposes that Eliphaz alludes to the oracle respecting the weakness and perishing condition of men.

2.—The sense of this verse is, that the fool brings himself to destruction by the indulgence of anger, and the credulous or simple, by his outrageous zeal and violence.—*Indignation.*—See Deut. xxix., v. 19.—*Simple.*—Noyes and Good: "the weak man." Walton: "the busy-body." Sept.: "the erring."

3.—*The fool taking root.*—I have seen the wicked prospering for a time, but I knew that calamity would soon follow. He refers here to Job's own case.—*Marked his abode.*—See Ezra viii., v. 20; Amos vi., v. 1. Dathe: "I presaged his sudden destruction."

4.—*Far from safety*—Who could feel this more than Job?—*Crushed in the gate.*—The courts of justice were usually held at the gates of ancient cities.—*No deliverer.*—No advocate to plead their cause. The Targum: "They shall be crushed in the gate of hell, in the day of the great judgment."

5.—*To the very thorns.*—Houbigant, by altering a little the original, proposes to translate: "And the'r sheaves armed men seize." A very ingenious conjecture.—*And the thirsty.*—The Hebrew word "tzammim" is the same as "tzeme'im," *the thirsty.* which the parallelism undoubtedly requires. Rosenmüller, the Vulgate, and others nearly the same.

6.—*Truly affliction.*—The Vulgate: "There is nothing on the earth without a cause." This is the sense here. *Spring out of the ground.* The Sept: *from the mountains.* Eliphaz says that affliction does not come upon man from a *natural* cause.

7. For then man would be born to trouble,
　　As the bird-tribes are made to fly upward.
8. Therefore I would seek unto God,
　　And to God I would commit my cause,
9. Who doeth great things, inscrutable,
　　Marvellous things without number;
10. Who giveth rain upon the earth,
　　And sendeth water upon the pastures,
11. So that He raiseth the lowly on high,
　　And mourners are exalted to safety;
12. Who frustrateth the designs of the crafty,
　　So that their hands cannot accomplish their enterprise;
13. Who taketh the wise in their own craftiness,
　　And precipitateth the counsel of the froward;
14. They meet with darkness in the day time,
　　And grope at noon as if it were night;
15. But He saveth the desolate from their mouth,
　　And the needy from the hand of the mighty;

7.—*Then man would be born to trouble.*—It would fall upon him naturally and necessarily, without any determination or direction of a moral agent. He could neither prevent it by his piety, nor hasten it by his impiety.—*As the bird-tribe.*—So Good, Sept., Syr., and Arab. Professor Wolfsohn, Gesenius, and Umbreit: "Birds of prey." The Targum: "the sons of demons."

8.—*I would seek.*—Eliphaz advises Job to confess his sins, and, with humble submission, to submit his case entirely to God's righteous decision, and in verse 9 he gives his reason *why* he may confidently commit his cause to Him.

10.—The Targum: "Who gives rain on the face of the land of Israel and sends waters on the face of the provinces of the people." *Pastures.*—So Eichhorn and Wolfsohn.

12.—*Enterprise.*—The Targum: "Who made vain the thoughts of the Egyptians, who acted cunningly that they might do evil to Israel, but their hands did not perform the work of their wisdom."

13.—The Targum: "Who took the wise men of Pharaoh in their own wisdom, and the counsel of their astrologers he made to return upon them.—*The wise.*—The cunning.

15.—There is some difficulty in this verse. The Targum, Syr., Arab., and Vulg. read: "mechereb pihem," "*from the sword of their mouth.*" This reading is supported by several Hebrew MSS. of De Rossi and Kennicott. Durell, Michaelis, Doederlein, Dathe, and Boothroyd change the vowel points, and make from "mechereb" the *hophal participle* from "chareb," *to make desolate.* I have followed the latter.

16. Hence the poor hath hope,
    And iniquity stoppeth her mouth.——
17. Behold! happy is the man whom God correcteth,
    Therefore despise not thou the chastening of the Almighty;
18. For He bruiseth, and He bindeth up;
    He woundeth, and His hands heal.
19. In six troubles He will deliver thee,
    Yea in seven no evil shall touch thee;
20. In famine He will preserve thee from death,
    And in war from the power of the sword;
21. From the scourge of the tongue shalt though be hid,
    Nor shalt thou fear approaching devastation;
22. At devastation and famine thou shalt laugh,
    Nor shalt thou dread the wild beasts of the land;
23 For with the stones of the field shalt thou be in league,
    And the wild beasts shall be at peace with thee.
24. Thou shalt know that thy tent is secure,
    Thou shalt inspect thy cattle-stall, and miss nothing.

17.—*Behold.*—The word "hinne," *behold*, is wanting in the Syr., Arab., Vulg., and several Hebrew MSS.

19.—*Six—seven.*—Many.

20.—The Targum: "In the famine of Egypt he redeemed thee from death, and in the war with Amalek from the slaying of the sword."

21.—The Targum: "From injury by the tongue of Balaam thou wert hid among the clouds, and thou didst not fear the desolation of the Midianites when it came."

22.—The Targum: "In the desolation of Sihon, and in the famine of the desert, thou didst laugh; and of the camp of Og, who was like a wild beast of the earth, thou wert not afraid."

23.—The Targum: "Thou needest not fear because thy covenant is on tables of stone, which are publicly erected in the field; and the Canaanites, which are compared to the beasts of the field have made peace with thee." Good follows Reiske, who reads "beney" *sons*, or *produce* of the field, instead of "abney," *stones*. We must remember that it was spoken in Arabia, where rocks and stones abounded, and where—from that cause—travelling is very dangerous. The idea might then be that he would be permitted to make his way in safety.

24.—*Cattle-stall.*—Gesenius: "thou musterest thy flocks." The word "navecha" no doubt means the place where cattle are kept, as in a place of security from straying and from the attacks of wild beasts. Nearly all the commentators on this verse vary.—*And miss nothing.*—So Wolfsohn, Gesenius, Houbigant and others. Heath: "and shalt not be disappointed." Rashi nearly the same.

25. Yea, know that numerous will be thy seed,
   And thine offspring as the grass of the earth;
26. Thou shalt come in full age to the grave,
   As a shock of corn is gathered in its season.
27. Lo! this we have searched out. So it is;
   Attend! and know thou it for thyself.

CHAPTER VI.

1. Then Job replied, and said:
2. O that my grief were thoroughly weighed,
   And my calamity laid in the balance against it!
3. For now it is heavier than the sand of the sea;
   Hence my words are vehement.
4. For the arrows of the Almighty are within me,
   The poison whereof drinketh up my spirit,
   The terrors of God array themselves against me.
5. Brayeth the wild ass over the grass?
   Or loweth the ox over his fodder?

26.—*Shock of corn.*—He would not die before he was ripe for heaven—as the yellow grain is for the harvest.

27.—*Know.*—Reduce them to practice for thine own good.

2.—Job supposed his friends had not understood and appreciated his sufferings, and he desired that they would estimate them aright. before they condemned him. They would see that, bitter as his complaint had been, it was little when compared with the distress which occasioned it.

3.—*Vehement.*—The authorised version: "*Swallowed up*;" but nothing can be more absurd, than to make Job say: "his words were swallowed up" (*i.e.*, that he could not find words to express his feelings), at the very time he was expressing them in language the most forcible and vehement. Schultens: "tempestuous." Rosenmüller: "my words exceed due moderation." Gesenius: "Therefore were my words rash."

4.—*The poison.*—Poisoned arrows were used among the ancients with the object of securing certain death where the wound caused by the arrow could not produce it.

5.—*Grass.—Fodder.*—Both are here a figure of abundance and tranquility, such as the friends of Job enjoined.—*To bray* and *to low* are to be considered as expressions of grief and uneasiness. Job compares his friends to a wild ass, enjoying his food in silence, and to an ox perfectly satisfied with his grateful pasture. Happy themselves, they condoled not with him in his wretchedness, nor sympathised with him in his sorrow, but rather blamed his mourning as importunate clamor, and as if he had behaved himself towards God with insolence and impatience.

6. Can that which is insipid be eaten without salt?
   Is there savour in the white of an egg?
7. But the things which my soul refused to touch,
   Even they in my sickness are become my food.——
8. O that I might have my request,
   And that God would grant me my desire;
9. That God would resolve to crush me—
   Would stretch out His hand, and cut me off!
10. Then would I yet have the consolation,
    (And could exult over this unsparing anguish)
   That I have not violated the commandments of the Holy One.
11. What is my strength that I should hope?
    What is mine end that I should prolong my life?
12. Is my strength the strength of stones?
    Is my flesh of brass?
13. Because I am without help,
    Should safe counsel be driven from me?

6.—Job says that there was a reason for his complaints, as there is a reason for adding salt to insipid food. See Dr. Russel's "Natural History of Aleppo," p. 27, and Rosenmüller, "Alte und neue Morgenland" on Gen. xviii., v. 6.—*In the white of an egg.*—There is great variety of interpretation with respect of these words. Sept. : " Is there any relish in vain words?" Jerome : "Can any one relish that which, when tasted, produces death?" He had no doubt a different reading. The Arab. : " In the juice of purslain." Gesenius the same. He says that *purslain* was proverbial for its insipidity among the Arabs.

9.—*To crush me.*—To put him to death, so as to release him from his sorrows. The Targum : " Let God, who has begun to make me poor, loose his hand and make me rich."

10.—*Exult.*—The Targum : " And I will exult when fury comes upon the wicked." I believe the sense here is, that were he permitted now to die, he would have the consolation of not having violated God's word.

11.—*Hope.*—To be able to sustain the trials much longer.—*What is mine end?*—What is *likely to be* mine end?

12.—*Strength of stones.*—To bear up against these accumulated trials. So Sicero : " For man is not chiselled out of the rock, nor cut from a tree; he has a body, he has a soul; he is actuated by mind, he is swayed by senses." Qua. Acad. iv., 31.

13.—Good : "Alas! there is no help in me!"

14. Shame on him who despiseth his friend!
He indeed hath departed from the fear of the Almighty.
15. My friends are faithless as a brook,
As streams of the valley that pass away;
16. Which are turbid by reason of the ice,
In which the snow is dissolved;
17. In the time when they become warm they vanish,
When hot they are consumed from their place;
18. The paths of their course are diminished;
They ascend in vapour, and are lost.
19. The caravans of Tema anxiously look;
The companies of Sheba eagerly expect them;
20. They are ashamed that they have trusted in them;
They come thither, and are disappointed.

14.—I have followed Good. This rendering is confirmed by thirty-two Hebrew MSS. of Kennicott and De Rossi, who read: "lemoes" "*to him that despiseth.*" The Vulg.: "He who takes away mercy from his friend, hath cast off the fear of the Lord."

15.—*As a brook.*—As a torrent, which rushes with great violence through its channel, and is often dried up when wanted. So Job, who expected condolence from his friends, was disappointed by them.

16.—*Of the ice.*—When it melts and swells the stream.

17.—*Warm.*—Gesenius and Noyes: "Narrow." Sept.: "Melting at the approach of heat." Jerome: "in the time in which they are scattered." The Targum: "In the time in which the generation of the deluge sinned, they were scattered." The word "Zarab" occurs nowhere else.—*Consumed.*—Dried up.

18.—*Diminished.*—Good: "The caravans turn aside to them on their way." Noyes: "The outlets of their channels wind about." Jerome: "Involved are the paths of their steps." Rosenmüller: "The bands of travellers direct their journey to them." I believe the idea is that the channels of the stream wind along until they diminish and vanish.

19.—*Caravans.*—*Companies.*—These were the caravans that went from Arabia Felix with merchandise to Egypt. Their road lay through Arabia Petræa, Job's country. The yearly caravan, which goes from Grand Caïro to Mecca, near Arabia Felix, passes the same way. Professor Wolfsohn: "The Pilgrims of Sheba."—*Anxiously look.*—They come with the expectation of finding the means of allaying their thirst. Tema, being the country of Eliphaz, the image would be well understood by him.

21. So now are ye become like it;
    Ye see my abasement, and are afraid.
22. Have I ever said: "Bestow on me a favour?"
    Or: "From your substance present a gift?"
23. Or: "Deliver me from the hand of the enemy?"
    Or: "Redeem me from the power of oppressors?"——
24. Instruct me, and I will be silent;
    And prove to me wherein I have erred!
25. How forcible are just arguments!
    But how doth your reasoning convince?
26. Do you consider your speeches convincing,
    And the words of one desperate but as wind?
27. Then on the helpless ye could fall,
    And dig a pit for your friend!
28. Now therefore be pleased to look on me;
    I stand in your presence; am I found false?
29. Consider, I pray; be not unjust;
    Yea, consider it yet again; righteousness may be in me.
30. Consider if there is any falsehood in my tongue;
    If my palate cannot discern perverse things!——

VII. 1. Alas! the life of man is a warfare upon earth,
    And his days are as the days of an hireling.

21.—*Like it.*—The torrent disappoints the caravans, Job's friends disappointed him. They brought him no consolation in his troubles.—*My abasement.*—From eminence into want and misery.—*Afraid.*—To approach me, lest I should apply to you for relief.

22-23.—Job says that he never called on them for assistance, they had therefore no reason to afflict him further by their reflections.

25.—*How forcible.*—The Targum and two Hebrew MSS. read: "Nimletsu," *how pleasant.*

26.—Good: "Would ye then take up words for reproof? The mere venting the moans of despair?" Heath: "Do you devise speeches to insult me? and the words of him that is desperate, are they as the wind?"

30.—Heath: "Must there needs be perversity in my tongue, because my palate cannot relish misery?"—*If my palate.*—Whether my moral taste is so far depraved that I can no longer distinguish "perverse things," or things that are contrary and opposite; such as truth and falsehood; justice and iniquity; happiness and misery.

1.—*Man.*—Miserable man.—*Warfare upon earth.*—So the Targum and Vulg. The Sept.: "Is not the life of man a place of trial upon earth?" Professor Wolfsohn: "Alas! mortal man has a host of sufferings upon earth." I believe this to be the idea here.

2. As a slave he panteth for the shade,
   And as an hireling he longeth for his wages;
3. So do I; I am made to inherit comfortless months,
   And wearisome nights are allotted unto me.
4. When I lie down then I say:
   " When shall I arise, and the night be fled ? "
   And I am full of restlessness until the dawn.
5. My flesh is clothed with worms and clods of dust;
   My skin is shrivelled, and become loathsome.
6. Slighter are my days than yarn;
   They are finished by the breaking of the thread.——
7. O remember that my life is but a breath;
   Mine eye shall no more see good;
8. The eye that hath seen me, shall see me no more,
   Thine eyes are upon me—and I am not!
9. As the cloud is consumed and vanisheth away,
   So he that descendeth to hades shall not ascend;
10. He shall no more return to his house,
    And his dwelling-place shall know him no more;

2.—*He panteth for the shade.*—See Deut. xxviii., v. 66, 67.

3.—*So do I.*—So do I pant for death. Rest and wages are the justifiable desire of the wearied labourer; ease and death equally so of the miserable. See Schultens.

5.—*Clods of dust.*—Accumulated on the ulcers which covered his whole body.—*Shrivelled.*—Rashi: "My skin is filled with wrinkles."

6.—*Yarn.*—" Oreg " is *not* the *weaver's shuttle*, but the *yarn*. Dr. Shaw, speaking of the eastern nations says: "The chief branch of their manufactures is the making of hykes or blankets, as we should call them. The women alone are employed in this work (as Andromache and Penelope were of old); *they do not use the shuttle*, but conduct every thread of the woof with their fingers." Now, if *shuttles* are not *now* used in the manufacturing of hykes, can we suppose that they were used in the time of *Job ?* Further, " Tikvah," though from the root " kavah," *to hope*, is it not also *thread, a cord, a string*, as in Joshua ii., v. 18-21? How true this sentiment!

7.—In the anguish of his soul, he turns his heart to God, and urges reason *why* he should close his life. Good considers " ruach " as a verb, and renders: "O remember, that if my life *pass away*, mine eye shall no more see good." Rashi observes: " Here Job denied the resurrection."

8.—*See me no more*—I shall be cut off from my friends.—*Thine eyes.*—Herder : " Thine eye will seek me, but I am no more."

11. Therefore I will not restrain my mouth;
    I will speak in the anguish of my spirit;
    I will complain in the bitterness of my soul.
12. Am I a sea, or a sea-monster,
    That Thou settest a watch over me?
13. When I say: "My bed shall comfort me;
    "My couch shall ease my complaint;"
14. Then Thou scarest me with dreams,
    And with visions Thou terrifiest me;
15. Hence my soul chooseth strangling——
    Death—rather than my present life.
16. I loathe it; I would not always live;
    Let me alone, for my days are vanity.
17. What is man that Thou shouldst bring him up?
    And that Thou shouldst set Thy heart upon him?
18. That Thou shouldst visit him every morning,
    And prove him every moment?

11.—*Therefore.*—All being hopeless I will indulge myself in complaining.

12.—The Targum: "Am I condemned as the Egyptians were, who were drowned in the Red Sea; or am I as Pharaoh, who was drowned in it in his sins, that thou placest a guard over me." Reiske translates "yam," *a buffalo*; Good: *a savage beast*. But is the sense here not clear enough, without giving an unusual meaning to the word "yam?" Job says: "Am I like the *sea*, which is ready to destroy the country, and therefore is imprisoned with bounds, or like a *sea-monster*, which must also be cooped up in the same way, that it may not have the power to destroy? I never gave evidence of such a disposition, and should therefore not be treated as a man dangerous to society."

15.— *My present life.*—The Hebrew literally "my bones." He was reduced to a mere skeleton. Herder: "Death rather than this frail body." Noyes and Rosenmüller translate it literal.

16.—Good: "No longer would I live! O release me! How are my days vanity."

17.—*Bring him up.*—Why dost Thou form man, take care of him in his infancy, and even to manhood; and then overwhelm with afflictions? This sense is more apposite here than "to magnify." The Syr.: "That Thou shouldst *destroy him*." Schultens: "That Thou shouldst *contend with* him."

18.—*Visit him.*—For the purpose of inflicting pain.—*Prove.*—By affliction.

19. How long ere Thou wilt turn from me,
And allow me to swallow down my spittle?—
20. Have I sinned, what shall I do to Thee?
O Thou Observer of Man!
Why hast Thou set me up as a mark for Thee,
So that I am a burden to myself?
21. Why dost Thou not pardon my transgression,
And take away mine iniquity?
For soon shall I sleep in the dust;
In the morning Thou shalt seek me,
And I shall be no more.

CHAPTER VIII.

1. Then Bildad, the Shuhite, spoke, and said:
2. How long wilt thou utter such things?
And the words of thy mouth be as a great tempest?

19.—*Swallow down my spittle.*—A proverbial expression among the Arabs, by which they understand: "Give me leave to rest a little after my fatigue." There is an instance which illustrates this passage in Hariri's Narratives, entitled "The Assembly." A person, who, being eagerly pressed to give an account of his travels, answered with impatience: "Let me swallow down my spittle, for my journey has fatigued me."

20.—*Have I sinned?*—An address to God. The Syr. and Arab. have the same translation. Kennicott contends that these words are spoken to *Eliphaz.* See his vindication of Job.—*A mark*—Why hast Thou made me such an object of attack? The Sept.: "An accuser of Thee."—*To myself.*—The Sept.: "To thee," and several commentators have copied this change. This is one of the passages which, according to the Masorites, were altered by transcribers. See Aben Ezra *in loco.*

21.—*Pardon.*—Admitting that I have sinned, why dost Thou not forgive me?

1.—*Bildad, the Shuhite.*—Shuah was one of the sons of Abraham, whose posterity was numbered among the people of the East, and his situation was probably contiguous to that of his brother Midian, and of his nephews, Sheba and Dedan. See Gen. xxv., v. 2, 3. Dedan, is a city of Idumea (Jer. xlix., v. 8), and seems to have been situated on the eastern side, as Teman was on the west. Ezek. xxv., v. 13. From Sheba originated the Sabeans, in the passage from Arabia Felix to the Red Sea. Sheba is united to Midian. Isa. lx., v. 6. It is in the same region however with Midian, and not far from Mount Horeb.

2.—*Such things.*—To murmur against God.—*The words.*—Syr. and Arab.: "The spirit of pride fill thy mouth." Sept.: "The spirit of thy mouth is profuse of words."—*Great tempest.*—So the Targum.

3. Doth God pervert judgment?
   Or doth the Almighty pervert justice?
4. Since thy children have sinned against Him,
   And He hath cast them away in the very act of their transgression;
5. Yet if thou wouldst seek early unto God,
   And make thy supplication to the Almighty,
6. If thou wert pure and upright,
   Even now would He arouse Himself for thee,
   And make prosperous thy righteous habitation.
7. Though thy beginning be small,
   Yet thy latter end would greatly increase.
8. For inquire, I pray, of the former generation,
   And search out the experience of their fathers;
9. For we are but of yesterday, and know nothing,
   Like the shadow are our days upon earth;
10. Shall they not teach thee, and tell thee,
    And utter these words from their hearts?
11. " Can the paper-reed grow without mire?
    " Can the bulrush grow without water?
12. " Even yet in its greenness, and uncut,
    " It withereth before any other herb."
13. Such is the fate of all who forget God;
    So perisheth the hope of the profligate.
14. His support shall rot away,
    And his trust shall be a spider's web;
15. He may lean on his web, but it shall not stand;
    He may grasp it, but it shall not endure.

4.—*Since.*—Bildad takes it for granted that his children had sinned.—*In the very act.*—The Targum: "He sent them off to the place of their transgression."

7.—See Ch. xlii., v. 12.

9.—*But of yesterday.*—We are of short life.

10.—*From their hearts.*—The fruit of careful and long experience.

11.—*Paper-reed.*—Papyrus Nilotica. Sept.: "Papyrus."--*Bulrush.*—" Achu," according to Gesenius, an Egyptian word, signifying *marsh-grass, reeds, bulrushes*, everything which grows in wet ground.

13.—This is the moral application of the comparison.

14.—*Rot away.*—So Good. The foundation on which he trusts shall rot away.

16. He is full of sap in face of the sun,
    And his branch shooteth forth over his garden.
17. About the heap of stones his roots are entwined,
    They look to the pile of stones.
18. Yet He shall absorb it from its place,
    Shall refuse to own it, saying: "I never saw thee!"
19. Lo! such is the joy of his course!
    And from the dust other shall spring up!
20. Behold, God will not cast away a perfect man;
    Nor will He lend His aid to the wicked.
21. Even yet may He fill thy mouth with laughter,
    And thy lips with triumph.
22. They that hate thee shall be clothed with shame,
    And the tent of the wicked be no more.

CHAPTER IX.

1. Then Job answered, and said:
2. Truly I know that thus it is!
    And how can man be just before God?
3. If He chooseth to contend with him,
    He cannot answer Him to one charge of a thousand.

16.—*In the face.*—The Targum: "Before the rising of the sun," *i.e.*, He is flourishing before the sun riseth, but he cannot bear its heat and withereth away.

17.—The Sept: "He sleeps on a heap of stones, and he lives in the midst of flint-stones." There is a great diversity of opinion in the interpretation of this passage. The comparison is, I believe, that the piety of the profligate is not planted in a rich soil. His heart is hard as a rock.

18.—The sense here is that the wicked shall wholly be destroyed. The figure of the *tree* is still retained.

19.—*Joy of his course.*—A strong irony.

21.—*Even yet.*—So Michaelis. This insinuates that if Job repented God might restore him to prosperity.

2.—*Truly I know.*—He alludes to the remark:—"Doth God pervert judgment?"

3.—*Answer Him.*—Good: "He could not acquit himself," making *man* both the object and nominative of the verb. But his rendering is not supported by the sense of the verb, or the idiom of the language.

4. Wise in heart! and mighty in strength!
   Who can resist Him and prosper?
5. Who removeth the mountains—
   Who overturneth them in His anger,
   And they know it not;
6. Who shaketh the earth out of her place,
   And the pillars thereof tremble;
7. Who commandeth the sun, and it shineth not,
   And sealeth up the stars;
8. Who alone stretcheth out the heavens,
   And walketh upon the high waves of the sea;
9. Who made Arcturus, Orion,
   The Pleiades, and the Chambers of the south;
10. Who doeth great things, inscrutable,
    Yea, wonders beyond number.
11. Lo! He passeth by me—and I see Him not;
    He goeth on, but I perceive Him not;
12. Lo! He taketh away, who can hinder Him?
    Who can say to him: "What doest Thou?"

4.—Herder: "Even the wise and the powerful. Who hath withstood him and prospered?" But I believe that it refers to God. Job says that God so well understood the whole ground of debate, and could so successfully meet all that could be alleged, that it was useless to attempt to hold an argument with Him.

5.—*Removeth the mountains.*—Changes which occur in violent convulsions of nature.—*Know it not.*—A Hebraism, meaning *suddenly, unexpectedly.*—Good: "And they have no trace."

7.—*Sealeth up the stars.*—God hides from our view the stars by the interposition of clouds.

8.—*High waves.*—One Heb. MS. reads "ab," *cloud,* instead of "yam," *sea,* which would be confirmed by Isa. xiv., v. 14. Houbigant adopts this as the genuine reading, though most critics adhere to the text. Scott renders: "noteh,"—*boweth.* Homberg the same. Sept.: "Who walketh upon the sea as upon a pavement."

9.—I have followed the Auth. Vers., but as to the Hebrew words, they might as well have been applied to any of the other constellations.—*Chambers.*—Good: "Zones."

10.—The same sentiment is expressed by Eliphaz, ch. v., v. 9.

11.—*He passeth by me.*—Rather: "He passes *over* me," as in the majestic movement of the heavenly bodies over my head.

12.—A similar expression occurs in Daniel iv., v. 35.

13. God will not turn away His anger;
    The proudest stoop under Him;
14. How much less could I answer Him—
    Could I choose out arguments against Him!
15. Whom, were I just, I could not answer— —
    Or, should I make supplication to my Judge?
16. If I call will He then answer me?
    I cannot believe He will listen to my voice.
17. He, who with a tempest overwhelmeth me,
    And multiplieth my wounds without cause;
18. Who doth not suffer me freely to breathe,
    But hath filled me with bitter griefs.——
19. Should I appeal to strength, lo! He is mighty;
    If to justice, who would be a witness for me?
20. Should I justify myself, my own mouth would condemn me;
    I perfect? It would prove me perverse!
21. I perfect? I should not know my own soul!
    I should disown my very being!
22. This one thing I therefore affirm,
    That the upright and the wicked he alike destroyeth.
23. When the scourge slayeth suddenly,
    And laugheth at the sufferings of the innocent;
24. Then the earth must be given in the hand of a tyrant,

13.—The Sept.: "By Him the monsters which are under heaven are bowed down."—*Proudest.*—Literally: "The supporters of pride."

14.—Barnes has given a new turn to this passage; he renders: "Truly if I should answer Him, I would carefully select my words before Him."

17.—The Targum, Syr., and Arab.: "He powerfully smites even every hair of my head, and multiplies my wounds without cause."

19.—*A witness for me.*—So the Targum and Houbigant. The Syr. reads: "Ammits *hoo*," instead of "hinneh." I believe this is the genuine reading.

20.—*I perfect.*—Should I attempt to maintain such an argument, the very attempt would prove that my heart is perverse and evil.

21.—The Sept.: "I have been guilty of impiety, I was not conscious of it; but yet the enjoyment of my life is taken from me."

24.—Good: "The earth is given over to the hand of injustice; she hood-winketh the faces of its judges. Where every one liveth, is it not so?" But the Hebrew will not bear out the rendering of the

Who covereth the face of its judges;
If this be not so, where—who is he?
25. Swifter than a runner are my days;
They flee away, they see no good;
26. They pass on like the reed-skiffs;
As the eagle darting upon his prey.
27. When I say, "I will forget my complaining,
" I will lay aside my anger, and look cheerful;"
28. Then I am in dread of all my sorrows;
I know that Thou wilt not acquit me.
29. I must be accounted wicked;
Why then should I labour in vain?
30. Should I wash myself with snow-water,
And cleanse my hands with soap;
31. Yet wouldst Thou plunge me in the ditch,
And mine own clothes would abhor me.—
32. For I could not, man as I am, answer Him,
Should we come together in judgment.

---

last sentence.—*Of its judges.*—Of the *righteous* judges, or, He blinds the judges, so that they cannot perceive right from wrong, nor administer justice with impartiality.—*Where—who is he.*—If this be not the case, *who* is he that acts in this way, and *where* is he to be found? The Syr. and Arab.: "Who can bear His indignation?"

25.—The Targum: "My days are swifter than the shadow of a flying bird."—*They see no good.*—My life is a life of misery.

26.—*Reed-skiffs.*—The Targum: "Ships laden with the best fruits." Vulg.: "Ships freighted with apples." Arab.: "Ships well adapted for sailing." The Syriac and forty-seven MSS. of Kennicott and De Rossi read: "Oniyoth eybah," *hostile ships.* The idea would then be that his days are gone like the light vessels of *the pirates*, having stripped him of his property, and carried every thing away under the strongest press of sail so as to effect their escape and secure their booty. The second part of the verse seems to confirm this reading.

28.—*Sorrows.*—I dread the continuance of my griefs.

29.—*Labour in vain.*—To justify myself.

30.—*Soap.*—So the Targum. The Hebrew word "bor" means (1) *pureness, cleanliness.* (2) That which cleanses—*alkali, ley,* or *vegetable salt.* The ancients made use of this, mingled with oil, instead of soap, for the purpose of washing or for melting metals.

33. Nor is there an umpire between us,
    Who can use his authority over both of us.
34. Let Him remove His supremacy from me,
    And let not the fear of Him terrify me;
35. Then would I speak, and not fear Him;
    But not thus, could I, in my present state.

X.

1. Weary am I of my very life,
   I will give myself up to complaint,
   I will speak in the bitterness of my soul.
2. I will say to God: " Do not condemn me;
   " Shew me wherefore Thou contendest with me.
3. " Is it a pleasure for Thee to oppress?
   " To despise the works of Thy hands,
   " And to shine upon the counsel of the wicked?
4. " Hast Thou eyes of flesh?
   " Or seest Thou as man seeth?
5. " Are Thy days as the days of miserable man?
   " Are Thy years as the years of man?
6. " That Thou seekest after mine iniquity,
   " And searchest after my sins,

33.—*Nor is there.*—Several Heb. MSS. of Kennicott and De Rossi, as also the Sept., Syr., and Arab. read: "lu yesh," *O that there were an umpire.*

35.—*But not thus.*—I am not able to vindicate myself in my present circumstances. I am now oppressed and crushed beneath a load of calamities; but if they were removed, and if I had a fair trial, I could justify myself.

1.—The Targum: " My soul is cut off." The sense is, that he himself was disgusted with life, and wished to die.

2.—*Do not condemn me.*—Do not hold me to be wicked, and do not treat me as such, without showing me the reasons *why* I am so regarded. Good: " Thou canst not unjustly deal with me." I do not think he is right in his rendering.

3.—*To shine.*—By giving them health and prosperity.

4.—*Eyes of flesh.*—Eyes of envy and hatred.

5.—*Are thy days.*—Dost Thou expect soon to die, that Thou dost pursue me in this manner, searching out my sins, and afflicting me as if there were no time to lose? The Auth. Vers. gives for "enosh" and "geber" the same rendering, *man*, but there ought to be a distinction. "Enosh" is *feeble, miserable* man; "geber" *strong* man.

7. " With Thy knowledge that I am not wicked,
  " And that none can deliver me out of Thy hand ?
8. " Thy hands formed me, and made me ;
  " Joined me together ; yet Thou wilt destroy me ?
9. " Remember, I pray, that Thou hast made me as clay,
  " And to dust wilt cause me to return !
10. " Didst Thou not pour me out as milk,
  " And curdle me as cheese ?
11. " With skin and flesh Thou didst clothe me ;
  " With bones and sinews Thou didst fence me ;
12. " Thou didst grant me life and favour,
  " And Thy care preserved my breath ;
13. " And these things Thou didst hide in Thine heart ;
  (" I know that this was Thy purpose ;)
14. " If I sin, Thou dost carefully observe me ;
  " And from mine iniquity Thou wilt not acquit me ;
15. " If I be wicked, woe unto me ;
  " If righteous, I cannot lift up my head ;
  " I am full of shame when I regard my affliction.

7.—*With Thy knowledge.*—Why dost Thou afflict me when Thou knowest that I am not wicked ? Why is occasion thus furnished to my friends to construct an argument, as if I were a man of singular depravity ?

8.—*Thine hands formed me.*—It looks then like a caprice to bestow great skill and labour on a work, and then, without a cause, dash it in pieces.

10-12.—This is as just an account of the principles of the *embryo*, and of the several stages of its growth to a perfect *foetus*, as modern anatomy, with all its discoveries and improvements, can give us. On this subject the reader may consult " Dunglison's Physiology," vol. II., p. 340. On verse 11, Grotius remarks that this is the order in which the infant is formed—that the skin appears first, then the flesh, then the harder parts of the frame.

13.—Rosenmüller, Good, Noyes, and Scott are of opinion that this refers to the calamities which God had brought upon him.

14.—Reiske : " Have I utterly *fallen away*, that Thou made a mark on me ?"

15.—The Hebrew word "rech" must here be considered as the participle, and thus it yields a just and connected sense. The Targum and Syr. render it in the same sense.

16. " Roused as a fierce lion Thou dost hunt me,
" And again shewest Thy wonderful power over me;
17. " Thou renewest Thy plagues against me,
" And increasest Thine indignation against me—
" Successive conflicts come upon me.
18. " Wherefore then didst Thou bring me forth from
" the womb?——
" O that I had expired, and no eye had seen me!
19. " That I were as though I had never been!
" That from the womb I had been borne to the grave!
20. " Are not my days few? Cease then,
" Let me alone, that I may have a little comfort,
21. " Before I go, and shall no more return,
" To the land of darkness and death-shade—
22. " To the land of gloom like midnight darkness;
" Of death-shade, and without order;
" Where the light is as midnight darkness."

CHAPTER XI.

1. Then Zophar, the Naamathite, spoke and said:
2. Shall not one multiplying words be answered?
 Or shall a vain babbler be justified?

16.—*Roused.*—This is an admirable picture of the sport which lions, and indeed all the feline tribe exercise over their prey before they finally devour it.

17.—*Increasest.*—Heath: "Thou devisest an army of new torments against me."

20.—*Are not my days few?*—Let then not my affliction be continued to the last moment of life, but let me have a little respite. Boothroyd would translate: "Will then my few days never cease?"

21, 22.—We have not the means in the English language of marking different degrees of obscurity with the accuracy with which the Hebrews did it.—*Without order.*—Having no arrangements, no distinction of inhabitants. Poor and rich; master and slave; king and beggar, all are there equal.

1.—*Zophar the Naamathite.*—Among the cities which by lot fell to the tribe of Judah, in the neighbourhood of Idumea, Naamah is enumerated (Joshua xv., v. 41); but this name does not occur elsewhere. It was probably the native place or residence of Zophar.

2.—*Vain babbler.*—Literally "a man of lips," a Hebraism, denoting a great talker. Reiske: " *To multiply words* " (in the infinitive) " answers nothing, or else would a man of talk be justified."

3. Shall thy vaunting make men silent?
Or shalt thou deride, and none put thee to shame?
4. For thou hast said "My conduct hath been right,
"And I am pure in Thine eyes."
5. But O that God would speak!
That He would open His lips against thee;
6. That He would shew thee the secrets of wisdom;
For they far exceed the most perfect knowledge:
Thou wouldst then know that God overlooketh many of thy sins.
7. Canst thou penetrate the decision of God?
Canst thou fathom the sublime design of the Almighty?
8. The heights of heaven—how canst thou attain?
That which is deeper than hades—how canst thou know?
9. The measure of which is longer than the earth,
And broader than the sea?
10. If He arrest, and imprison, and bring to trial,
Who can prevent Him?

3.—*Thy vaunting.*—Rosenmüller: "Should men hear thy boasting with silence?" Vulg.: "Shall man be silent for thee alone?" The Sept. render the whole passage: "He who speaketh much should also hear in turn, else the fine speaker thinketh himself just. Blessed be the short-lived offspring of woman!! Be not profuse of words, for there is no one that judgeth against thee, and do not say that I am pure in works, and blameless before Him." I am unable to understand how this could be made out of the Hebrew, nor do I understand the sense of their rendering. The rendering of the Auth. Vers., too, is very harsh, and I do not believe that Zophar charged Job with *uttering lies.*

4.—*My conduct.*—So Good, and also the Sept., Syr., and Arab. Job never said anything about the purity of his *doctrine*, as rendered by the Auth. Vers. Zophar seems to refer to what Job had said: Ch. ix., v. 15, 25, 30, and ch. x., v. 7.

6.—*Secrets of wisdom.*—The counsels of God, that fix the kind and measure of his punishments.—*For they exceed.*—The expression as it stands in the Auth. Vers. is not intelligible, and indeed it is difficult to attach any idea to it. Good, strangely enough: "For they are intricacies to iniquity," a meaning never before given the word "tushiyah." The sense is that they greatly surpass our comprehension.

10.—The Auth. Vers. does not explain the sense of the original. The Targum: "If He pass on and shut up the heavens with clouds," but the paraphrast did neither understand the passage. This verse refers to the ancient method of trying a criminal. First apprehended, then bound, the assembly called, and then the charges preferred. If God seize by some calamity, man becomes the prisoner of Providence, and then God makes a public example of him.

11. For He knoweth the false men,
   He seeth wickedness also; will He not notice it?
12. Let then the hollow-hearted be wise,
   And the colt of the wild ass become a man.——
13. If thou prepare thine heart,
   And stretch out thine hands toward Him;
14. If thou put away the iniquity of thy hands,
   And let not wickedness dwell in thy tents;
15. Then shalt thou lift up thy face without spot,
   Yea, thou shalt be steadfast, and shalt not fear;
16. Then shalt thou forget thy misery,
   Or but remember it as waters passed away;
17. And thine age shall be clearer than the noon-tide;
   Darkness itself shall become as the morning;
18. And thou shalt be secure, because there is hope;
   Wherever thou lookest around, in safety shalt thou lie down.
19. Yea, thou shalt rest, and none shall frighten thee,
   And many shall entreat thy favour.

12.—The Targum gives *two* renderings: "An eloquent man shall become wiser in his heart, and the colt of the wild ass is born as the son of man;" or: "The wise man shall ponder it; and the refractory youth, who at last becomes prudent, shall make a great man." The wild ass is a striking image of that which is untamed and unsubdued. According to Schultens, "Let the colt of the wild ass become a man" is an Arabian proverb, which they explain by saying: "Let a man that is untractable, wild. and fierce, become docile, gentle, and humane. There is no end to the translations of this verse, and conjectures relative to its meaning.

13.—*Stretch out thine hand.*—In the attitude of supplication.

15.—*Thy face without spot.*—Thou shalt be cheerful. The Syr. and Arab. read "thy hands," instead of "thy face."

17.—*Thine age.*—The remainder of thy life.—*Darkness.*—The Targum and Syr. nearly the same: "And the darkness shall be as the Aurora." The idea is: "Thine affliction shall be converted into joy."

18.—*Lookest around.*—The Targum: "Thou shalt prepare for thyself a sepulchre, and shalt lie down in safety." Noyes and Gesenius: "*Now* thou art ashamed. *then* thou shalt dwell in quiet." Rosenmüller: "Thou are suffused with shame." I believe I have given the right translation. The verb "chaphar" does not only denote "to dig," but also "to search," "spy out," "look around." Deut. i., v. 22; Joshua ii., v. 2, 3; Job xxxix., v. 29.

20. But the eyes of the wicked shall fail,
    They shall find no refuge;
    Their hope is—an exhalation of breath!

CHAPTER XII.

1. Then Job answered and said:
2. No doubt but ye are the people;
   And wisdom will die with you!
3. Yet I have understanding as well as you;
   I am not inferior to you;
   For who knoweth not such things as these?
4. A derision to his friend am I——
   "He calleth on God, and let Him answer him!"
   Derided is the just, the perfect man.
5. Contempt for calamity is a feeling of those at ease;
   It is ready for them that slip with their feet;—
6. Peaceful are the tents of robbers,

---

20. —*Shall fail.*—They shall be wearied out by anxiously looking for relief from their miseries.—*An exhalation of breath.*—The *last breath* they breathe is the final termination of their hope.

2.— *Ye are the people.*—A strong irony; as if he had said: "Certainly you are the only people worth listening to, and when you die, wisdom shall be no more."—Houbigant would read "tumas" *perfection*, "And with you is the *perfection* of wisdom." This also yields a good sense, understood ironically.

4.—*He calleth on God.*—Job repeats this as an instance of the derision which he had experienced from his friends. Eliphaz had insulted him by saying (ch. v., v. 1): "Call now, is there any one who will answer thee? And to which of the Holy Ones wilt thou appeal?" And Zophar had just uttered this bitter invective against him (ch. xi., v. 5): "O that God would speak! that He would open His lips against thee!" sneering at him for his appeal to God, Ch. x., v. 2. There has been considerable variety in the interpretation of this verse.

5.—There is much difficulty in this passage, and it has by no means been removed by the labour of critics. I believe the general sense is tolerably clear, but to *emendations* and *conjectures* there is no end.

6.—Here again we meet with a most difficult passage. Noyes: "Who carry their God in their hand." Eichhorn, Wolfsohn, and Stuhlman: "Who regard their fist as their God." Good: "Of Him who hath created *all these things* with his hand." He reads "Elch" *these*, instead of "Eloha" *God*. Sept.: "Who provoke the Lord as

And secure to those who provoke God,
Into whose hands God bringeth abundance.
7. But ask now the beasts, and they will teach thee ;
Or the fowls of the air, and they will tell thee ;
8. Or the herb of the earth, and it will inform thee ;
Or the fishes of the sea will declare it to thee ;
9. Who among these knoweth not
That the hand of the Lord hath done this ?
10. In whose hand is the life of every thing that liveth,
And the breath of all human flesh.—
11. Doth not the ear try the words,
As the palate tasteth its food ?——
12. With the aged is wisdom ;
And in the length of days, understanding.
13. " With Him are wisdom and strength ;
" To Him belong counsel and understanding ;

---

if there would be no trial to them hereafter ;" which makes sense, but it was never obtained from the Hebrew text. I have followed the A. V., which is as near as possible in accordance with the original. Job says God does not treat men according to their real character. The wicked prosper ; the righteous are afflicted.

7.—The object of Job is to show that rewards and punishments are not distributed according to character. It was seen even in the brute creation. Everywhere the strong prey upon the weak ; the fierce upon the tame ; yet God does not come forth to destroy the lion and the hyeana, the eagle and the vulture, and to protect the tender and harmless.

8.—*The herb of the earth.*—" Siach," *herb*. This appeal to the *herb* of the earth means that the same thing is shown in the productions of the earth, as in the case of fierce animals. Noxious weeds and useless plants are more thrifty than the plants which are useful, and the growth of poisonous or annoying things on the earth illustrates the same dealings of God with men—that his dealings are not in accordance with the real nature of objects.

9.—*Of the Lord.*—This is no doubt an *error* of transcribers. Several Hebrew MSS. read " Eloha," *God*.

10.—*Human flesh.*—This is more in accordance with the Hebrew.

11.—Job says that attention ought to be paid to the signification of words, as one tastes his food ; but his friends had not given that attention to his remarks.

13.—From here until the end of the chapter are the maxims of the wise.

14. " Lo! He pulleth down, and none can rebuild;
"He shutteth up a man, and none can release;
15. " Lo! He restraineth the waters, and they are dried up;
"He sendeth them forth, and they inundate the
" earth;
16. " With Him are strength and perfection;
" The deceived and the deceiver are His;
17. " He misleadeth counsellors to foolish designs,
" And judges He maketh fools;
18. " He looseth the bond of kings,
" And with a girdle He bindeth their loins;
19. " He leadeth princes away captive,
" And overthroweth the mighty;
20. " He depriveth orators of their eloquence,
" And the discretion of the aged He taketh away;
21. " He poureth contempt upon the nobles,
" And the girdle of the valiant He looseth;
22. " The recesses of darkness He exposeth,
" And bringeth death-shade to light;
23. " He increaseth nations, and destroyeth them;
" He enlargeth nations, and giveth them rest;

14.—*Shutteth up.*—The Targum: "He shuts up a man in the grave, and it cannot be opened." The idea is that God has complete control over man.

15.—It is remarkable that in the argument here there is no illusion to any *historical* fact; not to the flood, nor to the destruction of Sodom, or the passage through the Red Sea; though these occurrences would have furnished appropriate illustrations to the point under discussion, a strong proof of the antiquity of the book.—*Inundate the earth.*—Such inundations may have occurred in the swollen torrents of Arabia.

16.—*The deceiver.*—This signifies any foolish or wicked ruler, who, by his misconduct, brings ruin on his country. The *deceived* are the people so ruined. God overrules both, to serve the wise ends of his providence.

17.—*Fools.*—He leaves them to distracted and foolish plans. Nothing has been more frequently illustrated in the history of nations.—*Quem Deus vult perdere prius dementat.*—"When God purposes to destroy, He first infatuates."

18.—*The bond of kings.*—Their authority; and bindeth them, like slaves, to the triumphal car of their enemies.

20.—*Of the aged.*—The term "Zakan" includes two ideas, *seniority* and *official authority.*

24. " He taketh away prudence from the chiefs of the
" earth,
 " And causeth them to wander in a pathless desert;
25. " They grope in the dark without light;
 " He maketh them to reel like the drunkard."

XIII

1. Lo! all this mine eye hath seen;
 Mine ear hath heard and understood it.——
2. What ye know, I also know;
 I deem not myself inferior to you.
3. Would that I could speak to the Almighty,
 That I could reason with God!
4. But what varnishers of falsehoods are ye;
 Ye are physicians of no value!
5. O that ye would be altogether silent!
 And this indeed would be your wisdom.
6. Hear, I pray, my reasoning,
 And listen to the pleadings of my lips.
7. Will you speak wickedly on behalf of God,
 And argue deceitfully on behalf of Him?
8. Will ye be partial,
 Will YE contend on behalf of God?
9. Will it be good when He searcheth you out,
 If ye flatter Him as man is flattered?

1.—This verse ought not to have been disjoined from the former chapter. Several Hebrew MSS. read "kol eleh," *all this*, which may be accepted as the true reading.

3.— *Would that I could speak.*—His friends, he felt, were censorious and severe. They neither did justice to his feelings, nor to his motives. But he felt if he could carry his cause to God, He would do ample justice to him and his cause.——

4.— *Varnishers of falsehoods.*—The Chaldee verb, from which the Hebrew word "Tof'le" is derived, signifies *to plaster, to cover over.*— *Physicians of no value.*—They had come to give him consolation, but nothing that they had said had given him comfort.

5.—Compare my translation of Proverbs xvii., v. 28, and notes.

7.— *On behalf of God.*—Will you maintain unjust principles with a view of honouring and vindicating God?

8.— *Be partial.*—Will you, from partiality to God, maintain unjust principles?— *Will ye contend.*—Are *you* fit to be the advocates of God?

9.— *Searcheth you out.*—If He should investigate your *character*, and the *arguments* you adduced on His behalf. Houbigant: "Is it right for you to offer adulation to Him?"

10. Surely He will reprove you,
    If ye secretly be partial.
11. Should not His majesty fill you with reverence,
    And His dread fall upon you?
12. Your memorable sayings are dust,
    Your strongholds strongholds of mire.
13. Hold your peace, for I will speak,
    I will, and let what may come upon me.
14. Let what may—I will carry my flesh in my teeth,
    And put my life in my hand.
15. Lo! He may slay me, I expect nothing else;
    Still I will vindicate my ways before Him.
16. Yea, this also will become my salvation,
    That the impious will not so come before Him.
17. Hear ye with attention my speech,
    And listen to my declaration.
18. Behold, now I have ordered my cause,
    I know that I shall be acquitted.

11.—*Fill you with reverence.*—And restrain you from all presumptuous and unfounded reasoning.—*His dread.*—The fear of Him should cause you not to advance any sentiments which will not bear the test of examination.

12. Nearly all commentators vary. Heath: "Are not your lessons empty proverbs?" Good: "Dust are your stored-up sayings." Sept.: "Your boasting shall pass away like ashes." Noyes: "Your maxims are words of dust."—*Your strongholds*—Good: "Your collections, collections of mire." Buxtorf, Crinsoz, Heath, and others: "Your high-flown speeches." The idea is, that the arguments behind which they entrenched themselves were like clay, and could not resist an attack made upon them.

13.—*Let what may.*—Reproaches from you, or additional sufferings from God. One cannot but be reminded by this verse of the remark of the Greek philosopher: "Strike, but hear me."

14.—*I will carry my flesh.*—He would incur any risk or danger. This is a proverbial expression.—*And put my life in my hand.*—I will expose myself to danger. Compare 1 Sam. xxviii., v. 21.

15.—*I expect nothing else.*—I have translated according to the *Kethiv.* Reiske, Good, Heath, and Wolfsohn also adhere to the text. Rosenmüller, Houbigant, and the Ancient Versions read "lo" *to him*, according to the *Keri.*

16.—*Become my salvation.*—This also will cause my acquittal, because I can confidently appear before Him, which no impious man dare.

17.—Job here refers to his solemn declaration (v. 15-16), that he had unwavering confidence in God.

19. Who is he that will plead against me?
　　For then will I be silent—and die!
20. Two things only, O God, do for me,
　　Then will I not hide myself from Thy presence:
21. Withdraw Thy hand far from me,
　　And let not Thy dread make me afraid;
22. Then call THOU, and I will answer,
　　Or let ME speak, and answer Thou me.— — —
23. How many are mine iniquities and my sins?
　　Make known to me my transgression and my sins!
24. Wherefore hidest Thou Thy face,
　　And considerest me as Thine enemy?
25. Wilt Thou break a driven leaf?
　　Or wilt Thou pursue the dry stubble?
26. For Thou writest bitter things against me,
　　And entailest on me the sins of my youth;

19.—*Silent and die.*—Should any one prove that my course cannot be vindicated, then I will not speak one word more, and suffer death without further argument. The Authorised Version not only does not express the sense of the original, but exactly the reverse.

20.—*Two things.*—Job felt that he was now enfeebled by disease, and incapacitated from making the effort for self-vindication and for maintaining his cause which he would have been enabled to make in his palmy days.—*Not hide.*—I will stand forth boldly and maintain my cause.

21.—*Withdraw Thy hand.*—Remove my affliction.—*Thy dread.*—Do not so overpower me by Thy severe majesty, that I cannot present my cause in a calm and composed manner.

22.—*Call Thou.*—Be Thou the *plaintiff*, and I will enter on my defence, *or let me speak.*—Let *me* be the plaintiff, and commence the cause.

23.—Job seems to have been waiting for a reply, and seeing that he was waiting in vain, he opens the cause as the plaintiff or accuser. *Make known.*—Why I am thus punished.

24.—*Hidest Thou Thy face.*—To shew the light of His countenance, when applied to God, is considered as a mark of His divine favour and protection; "to hide the face" signifies the reverse—a proof of His displeasure.

25.—*Break a driven leaf.*—Wilt Thou pursue one so incapable of offering any resistance?

26.—Job seems to have been conscious of no other sins than the follies of his youth, and imagined that he was now suffering for them, which he thought was extremely hard.

27. Thou puttest my feet also in a clog,
   And Thou watchest all my paths ;
   Thou markest out the steps of my feet ;
28. And this to him who, as a rotten thing, wasteth away ;
   As a garment that the moth consumeth !

XIV.
1. Man—the offspring of woman,
   Few are his days, and full of trouble ;
2. He cometh forth like a flower, and is cut down ;
   He fleeth like a shadow, and abideth not.
3. Wilt Thou cast Thine eyes on such an one,
   And bring me to trial with Thee ?
4. Who can become pure from an impure thing ?
   Not one.——
5. Since then his days are fixed,
   The number of his months is with Thee,
   Thou hast fixed his bounds which he cannot pass :
6. Turn away from him, and leave him,
   Till he shall be satisfied like the hireling with his day.

~~~~~~~~~~~

27.—Perhaps Oriental researches will yet disclose some custom that will explain this verse. The various explanations given by critics do not satisfy me.

28.—Chaplow, Grey, and Heath transpose this verse after verse 2 of the next chapter. Good makes it the commencement of the 14th chapter.

~~~~~~~~~~~

3.—*Wilt Thou cast.*—Is one so weak, so frail, so short-lived, worthy of the constant vigilance of the infinite God ?—*Bring me to trial.*—Does God seek a trial with one so much His inferior, and so unable to stand before Him ?

4.—The Targum : "Who will produce a clean thing from man, who is polluted with sins, except God, who is One ?" Jerome nearly the same. Miss Smith renders : "Who is there pure, free from pollution." The idea here is, that Job pleads some mitigation of punishment from the consideration of man's depraved condition.

5.—*Fixed his bounds.*—Thou hast limited the time which he is to live, and he cannot go beyond it.

6.—*And leave him.*—The idea of "yechdal" is not *that he should rest*, but that God should *cease* afflicting him, or, in other words, leaving him to himself.—*Till he shall be satisfied.*—The verb "ratsah" never signifies *to accomplish*. Jerome : "Until his desired day shall come like that of an hireling." Sept. : "And comfort his life." Good : "That he may fill up his day." Noyes : "That he may enjoy his day."

7. For there is hope of a tree
 If it be cut down, that it will sprout again,
 And that its tender branch will not fail;
8. Though its root grow old in the earth,
 And its stock die in the ground;
9. Through the odour of water it may yet flourish again,
 And shoot forth boughs as when planted;
10. But man dieth, and wasteth away;
 Yea, man expireth—and where is he?
11. The waters from the lake fail,
 And the torrent is diminished and dried up:
12. So man lieth down and riseth not;
 Till the heavens be no more, they shall not awake,
 Nor be roused out of their sleep.—

7.—*Will not fail.*—It will spring up and live. This sentiment has been embellished by several authors. Thus Moschus on the death of Bion:

"Alas! the meanest flow'rs which gardens yield,
The vilest weeds that flourish in the field,
Which dead in wintry sepulchres appear,
Revive in spring, and bloom another year:
But we, the great, the brave, the learn'd, the wise,
Soon as the hand of death has closed our eyes,
In tombs forgotten lie; no suns restore;
We sleep, for ever sleep, to wake no more."

8.—The idea is, that though a tree is cut down, life remains in the *root*; but when man falls, life is wholly extinct.

9.—A fine metaphor. The water acts upon the decaying and perishing tree, as strong odours act on a fainting person.

10.—*Expireth.*—This is *all* the Hebrew word "Gava" means. The notion of giving up the spirit or the ghost—an idea not improper in itself—is not found in the Hebrew word.

11.—*From the lake.*—Not sea. The *sea* or *ocean* has never been dried up, so as to furnish a ground for this comparison. Herder supposes it to mean, that *till* the waters fail from the sea man will not rise again, but the Hebrew will not bear this interpretation. I therefore follow Noyes, and render "yam" *lake*, or a stagnant pool. The word "yam" is frequently applied *to a lake*. To the lake of Genesareth, Numb. xxxiv., v. 11; to the Dead Sea, Gen. xiv., v. 3; Deut. iv., v. 49; Zech. xiv., v. 8. It denotes the Nile, Isa. xix., v. 5; the Euphrates, Isa. xxvii, v. 1.

12.—*Till the heavens be no more.*—That is, never. This is the true interpretation of the passage, and this accords with its design. Job means to say, undoubtedly, that man would never appear again on earth; that he would not spring up from the grave as a sprout does from a fallen tree; that when he dies, he goes away never to return.

13. O that Thou wouldst hide me in hades;
   Wouldst conceal me till Thine anger be past;
   Wouldst fix a time, and remember me!
14. If a man die, O that he would live again!
   All the days of my warfare would I wait,
   Till my time to be relieved cometh!
15. Then Thou wouldst call, and I would answer Thee;
   Thou wouldst shew compassion on the work of Thy hands;
16. Thou who now numberest my steps,
   Wouldst then not watch over my sin;
17. My transgression would be sealed up in a bag,
   And mine iniquity tied up.——
18. But O! the falling mountain wasteth away,
   And the rock is removed from its place;
19. The waters wear away the stones,
   And floods wash away the soil of the land:
   So destroyest Thou the hope of man;
20. Thou overpowerest him for ever, and he departeth;
   Thou changest his countenance, and sendest him away.
21. His sons are honoured, but he knoweth it not;
   They are oppressed, but he perceiveth it not;

13.—*Hades.*—Not the *grave*, as the A. V.; it denotes the unseen world.

14.—The Targum: "If a wicked man die, can he ever live again?" Syr. and Arab.: "If a man die, shall he revive? Yea, all the days of his youth he awaits till his old age come." Sept.: "If a man die shall he live, having accomplished the days of his life? I will endure till I live again."

17.—*Sealed up.*—And Thou wouldst no more regard them.

19.—*The waters.*—By their constant attrition wear away even the hard rocks; they disappear and return no more.—*So destroyest Thou the hope of man.*—He dieth, never to revive again.

20.—*He departeth.*—For ever.—*Changest his countenance.*—A countenance—blooming as the rose—pale as the lily by death.—*Sendest him away.*—Never to return.

21.—*His sons are honoured.*—He is unacquainted with what is passing on the earth.—*Oppressed.*—And is not permitted to sustain them in their trials.

22. Only over him his flesh grieveth,
  And over him his breath mourneth!

Part 3.

CHAPTER XV.

1. Then Eliphaz, the Temanite, replied, and said:
2. Should a wise man answer with **arguments of wind**?
  And fill his bosom with the east wind?
3. Reasoning with words which cannot profit?
  And with speeches which can never avail?
4. Truly, thou casteth off reverence,
  And profanest prayer before God.
5. For thine own mouth teacheth thine iniquity,
  Though thou choosest the tongue of the crafty.

22.—This verse has been variously translated. The Targum: "Nevertheless, his flesh, on account of the worms, shall grieve over him, and his soul, in the house of judgment, shall wail over him." Another rendering of the Targum: "Nevertheless, his flesh, before the window is closed over him, shall grieve, and his soul, for seven days of mourning, shall bewail him in the house of his burial." Good: "For his flesh shall drop away from him; and his soul become a waste from him." Did this ingenious critic mean that as the flesh droppeth off, so his soul, his person, become a waste? or did he mean his *life* shall become a waste? Eichhorn: "His troubles pertain only to himself, his grief relates to himself alone." I have followed Scott; this is the true and best translation I have met with. In the daring spirit of oriental poetry, "the flesh" and "the breath" are made conscious beings; the former lamenting its putrification in the grave, the latter mourning of the mouldering clay which it once enlivened.

1.—*Arguments.*—The Hebrew word "da'ath" implies *argument*, as well as *science*, and gives us hereby a plainer meaning.—*Bosom.*—Good has proved by a variety of passages of Holy Writ, that the word "Beten," generally translated *belly*, implies the *upper* as well as the *lower belly*, the *chest* or *bosom*, as well as the abdominal organs; and the passage before us may be adduced as an additional proof of the truth of his opinion.—*East wind.*—This wind is vehement and noxious in Arabia. Eliphaz accuses Job of maintaining sentiments the most detestable and injurious.

3.—*With speeches.*—"With" is not in the original, but is confirmed by MSS., the Sept., and Syr. Houbigant also adopts the reading: "Bemillim."

5.—*Thine own mouth.*—Thy whole argument shows that thou art a guilty man, though thou hast used sophistical arguments to defend thyself.

6. Thine own mouth condemneth thee, and not I;
   Yea, thine own lips testify against thee.
7. Art thou the first man that was born?
   Or wast thou formed before the hills?
8. Hast thou hearkened in God's council,
   And hast thou reserved all wisdom to thyself?
9. What knowest thou that we know not?
   What understandest thou which we do not?
10. The aged and hoary-headed are with us—
    More venerable in age than thy father.
11. Are the consolations of God few to thee?
    Is there yet anything hidden from thee?

6.—*Thine own mouth.*—The sentiments which thou hast uttered show that thou art *not* a pious man.

7.—*The first man.*—Hast thou lived ever since the creation, and treasured up all the wisdom of past times that thou speakest now so arrogantly and confidently?—*Before the hills.*—The mountains and hills are often represented as being the oldest of created objects, perhaps because they are the most ancient things that appear on earth. See Psalms xc., v. 2; Prov. viii., v. 25.

8.—*Hast thou hearkened.*—Here God is represented in oriental language, as seated in a *divan* or council of state, where important questions are agitated and decided; and Eliphaz asks whether *he* had been admitted to that council, and had heard the deliberations. —*And hast thou reserved.*—Having obtained the secrets of that council, art thou now keeping it wholly to thyself?

10.—The Targum: "Truly Eliphaz the hoary-headed, and Bildad the long-lived, are among us; and Zophar, who is older than thy father." Job had admitted (ch. xii., v. 12) that "with the aged is wisdom;" and Eliphaz here urges that on that principle he and his friends had a claim to be heard. It would seem from this verse that Job was then not an old man.

11.—Scarcely any two translators or commentators agree in the *translation* or even *meaning* of this verse. Vulg.: "Can it be a difficult thing for God to comfort thee? But thou hinderest it by thy intemperate speeches." Sept.: "Thou hast been scourged lightly for the sins which thou hast committed; and thou hast spoken with an excessive insolence." Syr. and Arab.: "Remove from thee the threatenings (Arab.: *reproaches*) of God, and speak tranquilly with thy own spirit." Targum: "Are the consolations of God few to thee? and has a word in secret been spoken unto thee?" Houbigant: "Dost thou not regard the threatenings of God; or has there been anything darkly revealed to thee?" Good and Wemyss: "Are the mercies of God of no account with thee? or the addresses of kindness to thyself?" Rosenmüller, the second part of the verse: "And words most justly spoken towards thee?" I have conveyed in my translation, as near as possible, the sense of the original. For the meaning of the word "la'at" see 2 Samuel xix., v. 5.

12. Whither doth thy heart carry thee away?
    And what do thine eyes wink at,
13. That thou turnest thy spirit against God,
    And pourest forth such speeches from thy mouth?
14. What is man that he should hold himself pure,
    And, one born of a woman, that he should hold himself for just?
15. Lo! in His holy ones He putteth no trust,
    And the heavens are not pure in his sight;
16. How much less in abominable and corrupt man,
    Who drinketh iniquity like water!
17. I will now show thee, listen to me;
    And what I have seen I will declare;
18. Which the wise have told, and not hid,
    And which they received from their fathers;
19. To whom alone the land was given,
    And no stranger passed among them:

12.—*Thine eyes wink at.*—" The verb 'razam' is a transposition from 'ramaz,' *to wink at*, a not unusual occurrence in Hebrew."—RASHI. This verb has given considerable perplexity to commentators. Rosenmüller and Wolfsohn: "What mean thy rolling eyes?" Sept.: "Why are thine eyes elevated?" Schultens: "Why do thine eyes roll fury?" Luther: "Why art thou so proud?" I have followed Rashi, though the verb *may* convey the idea of pride and haughtiness. The word occurs no where else.

14.—*Hold himself pure.*—The Syr., Arab., and Wolfsohn give the Hithpael sense to the verb. I have followed them.

15.—*Holy ones.*—In ch. iv., v. 18, it is: "In His *servants*." The reference is to the angels.—*The heavens.*—The inhabitants of heaven, the angels.

16.—*How much less.*—How much *less* will He put trust in corrupt man; not "much *more*," as the Auth. Vers.—*Drinketh iniquity* — Wolfsohn: "Who thirsteth after iniquity as for water."

18.—The original is rather deficient in perspicuity, if not conveying a sense opposite to what the context requires.

19.—*The land*—The country where they dwelt.—*No stranger.*—No foreigner came to corrupt their sentiments by an admixture of strange doctrines. Eliphaz speaks like a genuine Arab, whose pride is his tongue, his sword, and his pure blood. It is possible, as Rosenmüller suggests, that Eliphaz means to insinuate that Job had been corrupted by the sentiments of the Chaldeans and Sabeans. See also Scott *in loco.*

20. " The wicked is all his days in anguish,
    " And during the few years allotted to the oppressor,
21. " A dreadful sound is in his ears :
    " In peace [he feareth] the destroyer might come
" upon him ;
22. " He dare not come out of the darkness,
    " For fear that the sword lieth in wait for him ;
23. " He wandereth abroad for food everywhere ;
    " He knoweth that a day of darkness is at hand ;
24. " Trouble and anguish fill him with dread ;
    " They seize him, as a king ready for the battle ;"
25. (For he hath stretched out his hand against God,
    He bade defiance to the Almighty ;
26. He ran upon Him with his neck,
    With the thick bosses of his shields ;
27. Because he covered his face with fatness,
    And made folds of fat on his flanks ;
28. Therefore shall he dwell in desolate cities ;
    In houses which no one will inhabit ;
    Which are ready to become a pile of ruins ;)
29. " He will not be rich ; his property will not remain ;
    " He will not attain his design on earth ;

20.—The Targum : "All the days of the ungodly Esau he was expected to repent; but he did not repent ; and the number of years was hidden from the sturdy Ishmael." Translators and commentators vary greatly as to the meaning of this verse. I believe my rendering, which is as near as possible in accordance with the original, will satisfy the indulgent reader, as conveying a good sense and connection.

23.—Sept : "He is destined to be food for vultures."

24.—*Ready for the battle.*—Whom it would be vain to attempt to resist.

26.—The translation of the Auth. Vers. is quite the reverse of the idea here. *Not* that he ran upon the neck of his adversary, or that he rushed against the shield of the Almighty—as would seem from the Auth. Vers.—but, that he ran in a haughty, confident manner, determined to overcome his foe, and rushes upon God *with* his *own* shield.

27.—*With fatness.*—He lived in luxury and excess.—*Folds of fat.* —The Arab. : " He lays Pleiades upon the Hyades." A proverbial expression for : " His ambition is boundless."

29.— *Will not be.*—He will not continue to be rich.—*His design.*— There is great difficulty in this part of the verse. Vulg.: "Neither

30. " He will not escape out of darkness ;
"A flame shall dry up his moisture,
"And he passeth away by the breath of His mouth."———
31. Let therefore, no one trust in vanity; he will be deceived;
Vanity will be his recompense.
32. It will destroy him before his time,
And his branch will not be green ;
33. He will cast off his unripe grape as the vine,
And shed his blossoms as the olive.
34. For the assembly of the impious will be solitary,
And fire consume the tents of bribery.
35. They conceive mischief, and bring forth vanity ;
And their bosom deviseth deceit.

CHAPTER XVI.

1. Then Job answered and said:
2. I have heard many such things as these !
Miserable comforters are ye all !

---

shall he send his root in the earth." Sept.: "And shall not cast a shadow upon the earth." Noyes: "And his possession shall not be extended upon earth." Wemyss: "Nor shall he be master of his own desires." Good: "Nor their success shall spread abroad in the land." Luther, nearly the same. Houbigant: "Neither shall his offspring be propagated upon the earth." Heath, adopting the Arabic derivation of the word by Schultens, reads: "Neither shall their prosperity take root in the earth." Gesenius supposes the word "minlom" (which causes the difficulty) to be corrupted.

30.—*Out of darkness.*—Out of calamity.—*Of His mouth.*—So Rashi and most commentators. Wolfsohn: "Of His *own* mouth." Boothroyd would read "keruach" *like* the breath of His mouth. A very ingenious reading.

32.—*Not be green.*—He will die without posterity.

33.—*Cast off.*—His children will not survive him, nor come to mature age.

34.—The *assembly.*—The family.

35.—*They conceive.*—They form and execute plans of evil.

2.—*Miserable comforters.*—They had come professedly to condole with him ; but all that they had said was adapted to deepen his distress.

3. Will the vain words ever have an end?
　　Or doth something urge thee to speak further?
4. I also could speak like you;
　　If ye were now in my place,
　　I could string together words against you;
　　I could shake my head at you.
5. But I would strengthen you with my mouth,
　　And the moving of my lips should assuage you;
6. But now, If I speak, my grief is not assuaged,
　　And if I forbear what am I eased?
7. Now that He hath wearied me!— —
　　Thou hast made desolate all my family;
8. Thou hast fettered me, which is for a witness;
　　And my leanness riseth up against me,
　　And accuseth me to my face.——

3.—*Vain words.*—Literally: "words of wind." This is a retort on Eliphaz, who had charged Job (xv., v. 2-3) with uttering only such words. The Syr. "Do not afflict me any more with speeches; for if you speak any more I will not answer you."

4.—*String together.*—Gesenius supposes that it means that he would make a league with words against them. Sept.: "Then I could insult you with words." Jerome: "I would console you with words." Good: "Against you will I string together old sayings." The idea is that there is no difficulty in finding arguments to overwhelm the afflicted. It requires no uncommon talent to do it, and he felt that he would have been fully competent for the task.

5.—*With my mouth.*—With that which proceeds from the mouth—words.—Good: "With my own mouth will I overpower you, till the quivering of my lips shall fail."

6.—*But now.*—If I attempt to vindicate myself, I am reproached; equally so if I am silent.

7.—Aben Ezra: "*My grief* hath made me weary." Jerome the same.

8.—This and the preceding verse are among the most difficult verses of this book, and no wonder that all the commentators vary. Noyes: "Thou hast seized hold of me, which is a witness against me." Wemyss: "Since Thou hast bound me with chains witnesses come forward." Good: "And hast cut off myself from becoming a witness." Luther: "He has made me skilfully and bears witness against me." Sept.: "My lie has become a witness" Jerome: "My wrinkles bear witness against me." Calmet joins this with the preceding verse. Houbigant and Wolfsohn do the same.—*For a witness.*—For an argument against my innocence. The fact that God has fettered me; that He has bound me as with a cord, is an argument for my friends as a proof of my guilt.—*Leanness.* Good: "calumniator." Jerome and Wemyss: "false witness." Sept.: "my lie."

9. His anger teareth me, and he pursueth me with hatred;
   He gnashed upon me with his teeth;
   Mine enemy darterth his eyes upon me.
10. They gape at me with their mouth;
    They smite my cheek reproachfully;
    They have conspired together against me.
11. God hath delivered me up to the ungodly,
    And hath cast me into the hands of the wicked.
12. Happy was I—but He hath crushed me;
    He hath seized me by the neck, and shaken me;
    He set me up as a mark for himself.
13. His archers compassed me around:
    The one pierced my reins, and did not spare;
    The other poured out my gall upon the ground;
14. The one stormed me with breach upon breach;
    The other rushed upon me like a warrior.
15. I have sewn sackcloth around my wounded skin,
    And defiled my head with dust;
16. My face is swollen with weeping,
    And death-shade is on mine eyelids;
17. Though there was no injustice in my hands,
    And my prayer was always pure.

9.—*His anger.*—Who that person is that is spoken of in this and the following verses, has been a question on which commentators greatly differ. Rosenmüller, Reiske, and others suppose that it refers to God. Rashi, Cocceius, Clarke, and others to Satan. Schultens, Good, and others to Eliphaz, as the leading man among his adversaries. I believe the connection requires the latter interpretation. The whole passage is a description of the manner in which Job supposed his friends had come upon him.

10.—Here he includes *all* his pretended friends.

11.—*Ungodly.*—*Wicked.*—His pretended friends.

15.—*Wounded Skin.*—So Kimchi and Wolfsohn.—*My head.*—Literally *my horn.* Syr: "My head." Targum and Rashi: "Glory." Homberg and Good: "Turban."—His head, which of late was so highly exalted, and adorned perhaps with the tiara, now hung down covered with sordid dust or ashes. See Bruce's Travels, vol. iv., p. 477.

16.—*Swollen.*—So Jerome, Wemyss, and Luther. Noyes and Wolfsohn: "Red." Good: "tarnished." Sept.: "*My belly is burned* with weeping."

17.—*Pure.*—Sincere, free from all hypocrisy.

18. O earth! cover not thou my blood!
 And let there be no hiding-place for my cry:—
19. Even now, behold, my witness is in heaven,
 And He who knoweth me is on high.
20. My friends may deride me;
 But mine eye languisheth for a judge,
21. Who will plead between man and God,
 As between man and his fellow-man.——
22. For my few years are come to an end,
 And I go the way whence I shall not return.

XVII.
1. My breath is corrupt; my days are at an end;
 The grave is waiting for me.
2. Are there not mockers with me?
 And is not mine eye fixed on their provocations?—
3. Appoint, I pray, my surety with Thee;
 Who else will strike hands with me?
4. For Thou hast hid their heart from understanding,
 Therefore Thou wilt not exalt them:

18.—*O earth.*—Aben Ezra, and after him Scott, Good, and others suppose that Job refers to blood *shed by* him; and that the idea is that he would have the earth reveal the blood if he had shed any.—But with all deference to these learned men, I do not see that this meaning can be supported by the Hebrew text, and I think the text is clear enough. He says: "Let my blood cry against my murderers."—Eichorn says, according to the sayings of the Arabs, the blood of one unjustly slain remained upon the earth without sinking into it, until the avenger of blood came up. It was regarded as a proof of innocence. *Hiding-place.*—Let there be nothing to hinder my cry from ascending to heaven.

22.—Wolfsohn connects this verse with the following chapter. Scott concludes this chapter after verse 1 of ch. xvii.

1.—*Corrupt.*—This is the Chaldee sense of the verb. His vital powers were nearly extinct.—*The grave.*—Hebrew "graves;" but why so used I know not. Schultens remarks that the *plural* form is common in Arabic Poetry.

2.—*Fixed.*—He had a calm view of their wickedness, and could not be deceived.

3.—Job addresses God, with whom he desires to enter into a judicial investigation, and to pledge Himself that justice would be done to him.—*Who else.*—Striking hands confirmed an agreement, and in no one else but God would he trust.

4.—*From understanding.*—They will not render me justice.—*Exalt them.*—By the honour of deciding a case like this.

5. The one by flattery denounceth friends,
   Though the eyes of his children should fail;
6. The other hath made me a byword of the people;
   I am an object of scorn before their face;
7. Therefore mine eye is dim with sorrow,
   And all my limbs are as a shadow.
8. The upright will be astonished at this;
   And the innocent roused against the impious;
9. Yet the righteous will hold on his way,
   And he of pure hands increase strength;
10. But as for you all, ye may depart, and come again,
    I shall not find one wise among you.——

5.—This is a most difficult verse. Schultens says this verse is "a gordian knot," hence all translators vary. Noyes: "He that delivers up his friend as a prey, the eyes of his children shall fail." Wemyss nearly the same. Good: "He that rebuketh his friends with mildness even the eyes of his children shall be accomplished." Sept.: "He announces evil for his portion; his eyes fail over his sons." Vulg.: "He promises spoil to his companions, and the eyes of his sons fail." Scott joins the first word of this verse with the preceding verse. The Syr. the same.

6.—*Scorn.*—Sept.: "I am become a laughter to them." Vulg.: "I am an example to them." Targum: "I shall be *gehenna* to them." Auth. Vers.: "Aforetime I was as a tabret;" a most unhappy rendering. The true signification of the word "topheth" is to be sought in the Arabic, and in that sense I have translated.

7.—*Mine eye is dim.*—Schultens supposes that this refers to his external appearance in general, as being worn down, exhausted, defaced by his many troubles; but it seems rather to mean that his eyes failed on account of weeping.—*As a shadow.*—I am a mere skeleton; I am exhausted and emaciated by my sufferings.

8.—*Astonished at this.*—That the good are afflicted in this manner. —*Roused.*—Because he will otherwise be led to disparage virtue, piety, and innocence, on account of my sufferings.

9.—*Yet the righteous.*—Job probably refers this *to himself*, it being a declaration that *he*, a righteous man, though he had been so grievously calumniated, would still hold on his way and increase in strength.—*Pure hands.*—Porphyry remarks (de antro Nympharum) that in the "mysteries" those who were initiated were accustomed to wash their hands with honey instead of water, as a pledge that they would preserve themselves from every impure and unholy thing. See Burder, in Rosenmüller's Alte und neue Morgenland, *in loco.*

10.—Heath and Houbigant: "Now therefore recollect yourselves. I pray you, all of you, and consider. Cannot I find one wise man among you?"

11. My days are passed; my plans are at end—
The cherished purposes of my heart.
12. Can they change night into day?
Can light be at hand when I am encompassed with darkness?
13. When I prepare my home in hades,
When I spread my bed in the place of darkness;
14. When to corruption I say: "Thou art my father,"
To the worm; "My mother, and my sister:"
15. Where is then my hope?
And my hope who will see fulfilled,
16. When my limbs descend in hades,
When together they will rest in the dust?

CHAPTER XVIII.

1. Then Bildad the Shuhite answered, and said:

11.—*My days are passed.*—I am about to die. Job relapses again into sadness.—*Cherished purposes.*—The purposes which he had hoped to accomplish. All these were now to be broken off by death. This is, to man, one of the most trying things in death. His projects of ambition and gain, of pleasure and of fame, of professional eminence and of learning, all are arrested midway. How many *unfinished* plans are caused by death every day! Soon, reader, all *your* plans and *mine* will be ended—mine, perhaps, before these lines meet your eye; yours soon afterwards.

12.—*Can they.*—He refers to his professed friends. By "night" he means *troubles.*

13.—*When I prepare.*—When I have no other expectation but to make my home in the grave.

14.—*To corruption.*—According to Schultens and Rosenmüller the word "shachath" has to be understood in the sense of corruption or putrification, and it constitutes a parallelism with "worm;" though Gesenius contends that the word never has the sense of *corruption.*—*My father.*—He was so diseased, that he could justly say he was the child of one mouldering in the grave.—*My mother.*—I am so nearly allied to the worms, that the connection may be compared to that of a mother and her son.

15.—*Where is then my hope?*—What possibility is there of my escape from death.

16.—*When my limbs.*—So Rashi, Kimchi, and Wolfsohn.—*Together.*—His limbs and his hopes. The attentive reader will observe that from verse 12 until the end of the chapter I am at variance with nearly all translators. A careful examination, however, will convince the indulgent reader that I have given a clear connection, without violating the original.

2. How long will it be ere ye make an end of words?
Use sound arguments, and then we will speak.
3. Wherefore are we regarded as beasts,
And reputed senseless in your sight?
4. O, thou who tearest thyself in thine anger,
Shall the earth be deserted for thy sake,
Or the rock removed from its place?
5. Yea, the light of the wicked shall be put out,
And the flame of his fire shall not shine forth;
6. The light will be dark in his tent,
And his lamp above him be extinguished;
7. His strong steps shall be embarrassed,
And his own plans shall cast him down;
8. Lo! he is cast into the net by his own feet;
He runneth to and fro in the toils;
9. The gin will take him by the heel;
The noose will prevail against him;

2.—*How long.*—Properly, the word "lo," *not*, should have been in the original after "anah."—*Ere ye make.*—According to some commentators, he addresses Job and Eliphaz, who were the most tedious in their remarks. According to others, he addresses Eliphaz and Zophar, for not having arrested Job in his remarks. Probably he addressed *all* those present.—*An end of words.*—Good: "How long will ye plant thorns among words." Castell, Schultens, and Michaelis, contend that "kintsey" is an Arabic word: "How long will ye put ensnaring words." I cannot agree with these critics. "Kintsey" is the Chaldee form for "kitsey," and the word "lemillin," *to words*, the *Chaldee* plural of the *Hebrew* "lemillim" shows that the verse is formed after the Chaldee model, and so I have translated.

3.—*As beasts.*—Having no sense. He refers to Job's words (ch. xvii., v. 4.)

4.—*O, thou.*—For this substitution of the vocative case see Ob. 3, 4., Hab. ii., 15, 16.—*Tearest thyself.*—Whilst treating *us* as senseless, *thou* art a furious maniac.—*Be deserted.*—Are you of so much importance, that the earth should be made vacant for you to dwell in?

6.—*The light.*—The Arabians often use this image. Thus they say: "Bad fortune has extinguished my lamp." See Schultens.

7.—*Strong steps.*—Literally "the steps of his strength," a Hebraism; *large steps* are proverbial expressions among the Arabs to denote *freedom, prosperity*, &c. See Schultens and Rosenmüller.

8.—*Lo.*—An exclamative, not a causative particle.—*By his own feet.*—He walks himself into it.

9.—Houbigant reads verse 10 before verse 9.

10. For its cordage lieth hidden in the ground,
    And a trap for him in the pathway.
11. Terrors alarm him on every side,
    And harass him at his heels ;
12. His strength shall be exhausted by hunger,
    And destruction ready at his side ;
13. It shall devour the skin of his limbs,
    The first-born of death shall devour his limbs.
14. His hope shall be rooted out of his tent,
    And he shall be brought to the king of terrors ;
15. Terror shall dwell in his tent—for it is no longer his ;
    Brimstone shall be scattered upon his habitation ;
16. His roots beneath shall be dried up,
    And his branch above shall wither ;
17. His memory shall perish from the earth,
    And he shall have no name in the street ;
18. He shall be driven from light into darkness,
    And chased out of the world.
19. He shall have no son or nephew among the people,
    Nor any survivor in his dwellings ;

11.—*Terrors.*—"Terrors" are here represented as allegorical persons, like the Furies in the Greek poets. NOYES.

12.—The Targum : "Let his first-born son be famished, and affliction be prepared for his wife." Rashi the same.

13.—*The skin of his limbs.*—Rashi's paraphrase : "It shall devour the other members of his family."—*First-born of death.*—The most destructive disease that death has ever engendered. Rashi : "The angel of death." The Targum : "The angel of death shall consume his children."

14.—*His hope.*—Rashi's paraphrase : "He will be taken away from his wife, whose hope he is, and she shall send him to the grave of the king of devils."—*King of terrors.*—The Targum the same. Sept. : "And distress shall lay hold on him, with the authority of a king," Vulg. : "Destruction shall tread upon him as a king." Good : "Dissolution shall invade him like a monarch." Noyes : "Terrors pursue him like a king." Schulteus and Wemyss : "Terror shall seize him as a king." There is one of De Rossi's MSS. which reads : "kemelech," *as* a king.

15.—*Terror.*—So Rosenmüller, Noyes, Wemyss, and Wolfsohn.— *No longer his.*—It is tenantless. Rashi's paraphrase : "His *widow* shall dwell in his tent, for he is dead."

17.—*No name.*—After his demise none shall talk of his *fame.*

20. The dwellers in the West shall be astonished at his day;
They in the East shall be struck with horror.
21. Truly such are the dwellings of the wicked ;
Such the place of him that knoweth not God !

CHAPTER XIX.

1. Then Job answered and said :
2. How long will ye vex my soul,
And crush me with words?
3. These ten times have ye reproached me ;
Ye are not ashamed to stun me.
4. And be it indeed that I have erred,
That mine error hath harboured within me,
5. Will ye then triumph over me,
And expose to myself my own disgrace ?
6. Admit therefore that God hath done injustice to me,
And hath enclosed me with His net.

20.—*In the West.—East*—This accords better with the scope of the passage than the rendering of the Auth. Version, and avoids some difficulties which cannot be separated from the rendering of the A. V. The word "Acharonim" (from "Achar," *after, behind*) denotes those who dwelt in *the West*. In the geography of the Orientals the face was supposed to be turned to *the East*, instead of being turned to *the North*, as with us, a much more natural position than ours ; hence the word "after" or "behind" comes to denote *the West ;* the right hand *the South*, the left *the North*. Thus "Yam hoacharon" denotes the Mediterranean Sea—the West ; Deut. xxiv., v. 3.—*In the East.*— "Kadmonim," from "Kadam" *to precede, to go before*. As the face was turned to the *East* by geographers, the word comes to express that which is in the East, or near the sun rising. Hence the phrase "bene kedem"—sons of the East—meaning the persons who dwelt East of Palestine. Job i., v. 3 ; Isaiah xi., v. 14 ; Gen. xxv., v. 6 ; xxix., v. 1.

3.—*Ten times.*—Many times. The exact arithmetical number is not to be regarded here. See Gen. xxxi., v. 7 ; Lev. xxvi., v. 26.— *To stun me.*—So Gesenius and Noyes. Wemyss : "To treat me thus cruelly." Vulg. : "Oppressing me." Sept. : "And ye are not ashamed to press upon me." The word "hakhar" occurs nowhere else, hence it is difficult to determine its meaning.

4, 5.—I have followed Good. Every critic ought to be obliged to this learned gentleman for thus seizing the spirit of the original.

6.—*Enclosed me.*—Bildad had said (xviii., v. 8) that the wicked would be taken in his own snares. Job says, that *God* had ensnared him.

7. Lo! I complain of violence, but am not heard;
   I cry aloud, but there is no justice.
8. He hath fenced up my way, that I cannot pass,
   And He hath veiled my path with darkness;
9. He hath stripped me of my glory,
   And taken the crown from my head;
10. He hath wholly destroyed me, and I am gone,
    And my hope He hath rooted up as a tree;
11. He hath also kindled His wrath against me,
    And regardeth me as one of His enemies;
12. His troops come on together;
    They entrench themselves against me,
    And encamp round about my tent;
13. My brethren He hath put far from me,
    And my friends are truly estranged from me;
14. My neighbours cease to own me,
    And mine intimate friends have forgotten me;
15. The sojourners in my house,
    Yea, my maids regard me as a stranger—
    I am an alien in their sight;

7.—*Violence.*—God had dealt with him in a severe and violent manner, and he had cried unto Him for relief, but had cried in vain.—*No justice.*—God would not interpose to remove the calamities which He had brought upon him, and *his friends* would do no justice to his motives and character.

8.—This figure is taken from a traveller, whose way is obstructed, and he cannot get along; so Job says it was with him. He was travelling on the journey of life, and all at once obstructions were put in his path, so that he could go no further.

9.—*Glory.*—*Crown.*—Metaphorical expressions, signifying his dignity, and the honours which he had been accustomed to receive from his fellow-creatures, in consequence of his authority, justice, and beneficence.

10.—*And I am gone.*—I can recover no more.—*My hope.*—Of life and happiness, and of an honoured old age is totally destroyed.

11.—*Regardeth me.*—The same complaint he makes ch. xiii., v. 25.

12.—*His troops.*—The calamities seem to be meant here. They are here represented as *soldiers*, to accomplish his work.

14, 15.—The division of these two verses should be:
    14. "My neighbours and friends cease to own me;
       "The sojourners in my house forget me;
    15. "My maids regard me as a stranger;
       "I am an alien in their sight."

16. I call my servant—but he answereth not,
   Till I entreat him with my mouth;
17. My breath is strange to my wife,
   And mine entreaties to the offspring of my mother's womb;
18. Yea, young children despise me,
   I rise up, and they speak against me;
19. All mine intimate friends abhor me;
   Those whom I loved are turned against me;
20. My bones cleave to my skin and flesh,
   And I am escaped with the skin of my teeth;

15, 16.—Here, the disregard and contempt usually shown to men who have fallen from affluence and authority into poverty and dependance, are forcibly described; formerly reverenced by *all*, now esteemed by *none.—My maids.*—The Targum : "My concubines."

16.—*Till I entreat him.*—Obedience has ceased.

17.—*My breath is strange to my wife.*—Her heart was not moved by his groanings. This seems to be the idea here. Most critics render "zarah" *loathsome, corrupt.* This would imply that Job makes an apology for his wife's disrespect, contrary to the design of the passage.—*To the offspring of my mother's womb.*—His brothers and sisters. The word "bitni" has the same meaning as in ch. iii., v. 10. Commentators are greatly puzzled with this verse, and but few have caught the meaning. The Sept. : "I effectionally entreated the sons of my concubines," a translation of their own imagination, because *that* the original never means.

18.—*Young children.*—So Rashi. Vulg. : "Fools." Good : "Dependents." Schultens thinks "the children of his slaves" are meant, those who had been born and brought up in his house. The Sept.: "They renounced me for ever." How this was made out of the Hebrew I know not.—*Speak against me.*—They calumniate me. For this meaning of the word "dabber" see Numbers xii., v. 1.

20.—*To my skin and flesh.*—In the parallel passage, Ps. cii, v. 6, the word "to my skin" is wanting, and I believe it ought to be omitted, as it is implied in the next term.—*With the skin of my teeth.*— This seems to be a proverbial expression, signifying that a person had been so mangled and disfigured as to have no sound part over the surface of his body. Critics and commentators greatly differ on the meaning of this expression. Homberg thinks that Job by this expression meant "his mouth," which is *the skin of the teeth* (or covers the teeth), as the skin covers the flesh, and that the idea is that, of his whole body, *his mouth* only remained intact, so that he could complain. Good renders : "And in the skin of my teeth I am dissolved." (The meaning of which I do not understand). Herder: "And scarcely the skin in my teeth have I brought away as a spoil." (This rendering the Hebrew will not bear). Schultens supposes that his teeth had fallen out by the force of the disease, and that nothing was left but the gums. Luther : "And I cannot cover the teeth with the skin."

21. Pity me, pity me, O ye my friends!
   For the hand of God hath smitten me.
22. Why do ye persecute me like God,
   And are not satisfied with my flesh?— —
23. O that my words were now written!
   O that they were inscribed in a book!
24. That with an iron pen and with lead
   They were cut into the rock for ever!—— -
25. Indeed I know that my Avenger liveth,
   And that at last over this dust He will arise;

22.—*Not satisfied with my flesh.*—Enough that my *body* is destroyed, why then labour to torment my *mind?* Schultens remarks that "to eat the flesh of another" is an Arabian phrase for calumniating him.

23.—*Inscribed.*—The translators of the A. V. have made a strange mistake by rendering "printed." In the days of Job printing was unknown; in fact the Hebrew verb has quite a different meaning. "Chakak" means *to cut in, to hew, to engrave, to cut* (a sepulchre) *in a rock*, &c.

24.—*With lead.*—Rashi, Castell, and others are of opinion that the text refers to the ancient practice of cutting the letters with a style or chisel first, and then filling up the strokes with molten lead, so that the record became more permanent. Others suppose that Job meant that the records should be made on plates of lead; but, though such plates were indeed used in early times, the Hebrew word as it stands will not bear that interpretation.

25.—No part of the Scriptures has given rise to more disputes or has exercised the talents of critics more than these three verses. The general belief of Christians is, that these verses refer to the founder of their faith, and to the resurrection of the dead. The Vulg. renders: "For I know that my redeemer liveth, and that in the last day *I shall rise from* the earth; and again I shall be enveloped with my skin, and in my flesh shall I see my God; whom I myself shall see, and mine eyes shall behold, and not another; this my hope is laid up in my bosom." The Vulg. has thus rendered as though the passage would refer to Job; but the original has been corrupted to bring out this rendering, for there we read: "yakum," *he will arise*, and *not* "akum," *I will arise*. The Sept.: "For I know that he is eternal who is about to deliver me, to rise again upon the earth this skin of mine which draws up these things." (The meaning of which I am not able to divine). "For from the Lord these things have happened to me of which I alone am conscious, which mine eye has seen and not another, and which have all been done to me in my bosom." The Syr. and Targum agree nearly with the Hebrew. The Auth. Version: "For I know that my redeemer liveth, and that he shall stand up at the latter day upon the earth. And though after my skin worms destroy this body, yet in my flesh shall I see God: whom I shall see for myself, and mine eyes shall behold, and not another; though my veins be consumed within me." From this translation it is evident that the translators supposed that it had a reference to the founder of their faith, and to the resurrection; hence they gave a force to their expression, and they allowed their feelings to give a complexion to their language which the original does not convey. They use here the word "Redeemer," which is technically used to denote the founder of their faith, though the same word "goël" is rendered by them "kinsman," Ruth iv., v. 1-3, 6-8; "near kinsman," Ruth iii., v. 9-12; "kin," Lev. xxv., v. 25; "avenger," Numb. xxxv., v. 12; Josh. xx., v. 3. Again, they make use of the technical phrase "at the latter day" (the resurrection), which, as will directly be seen, is *not* in the original. I shall first investigate the *words* and *phrases* which occur in these verses, to show that their notion cannot be supported by the original, and that it is repugnant to the whole tenor of the argument. *I know that my Avenger liveth.* The "goël," which I render "avenger," is introduced in the Holy Scriptures as having a right "to redeem a mortgaged field," Lev. xxv., v. 25, 26; as having a right as kinsman to the restoration of anything which had been iniquitously acquired, Numb. v., v. 8. The word "goël" is applied to God who had redeemed the Israelites from bondage, Exod. vi., v. 6; Isa. xliii., v. 1. The "goël" or nearest kinsman of one slain, had a right to pursue the murderer, and to take vengeance on him, as long as he was not in one of the "cities of refuge." The "goël" was thus an *avenger* or *vindicator of violated rights*, and here it refers to *God*, who would be the "goël," *the avenger* of the innocent Job. "I know that my avenger liveth," says Job. Similar to this he has expressed himself, ch. xvi., v. 19: "My witness is in heaven, and He who knoweth me is on high."—*And that at last.*—Auth. Vers.: "At the latter day." The word "day" is supplied by the translators. Now it needs no great knowledge of the Hebrew language to know that "acharon," as a noun, denotes *the last*, and, as an adverb, *at last*, but never *the latter day*. The idea so far is thus, that *at some future period* in the life of Job, God would come as the avenger of Job.—*Over this dust.*—Auth. Version: "Upon the earth." Had the author intended to convey the idea expressed by the translators of the A. V., he would certainly *not* have used the term "aphar," *dust*, but "erets," or "adamah." He had his reason *why* he used the term "aphar," *dust;* he meant *his body*, which is *of dust*. "Thou art *aphar*, dust," God said to Adam, Gen. iii., v. 19; "I am *aphar*, dust," said Abraham, Gen. xviii., v. 27.—*He will arise.*—The word "yakum," *he will arise*, is a judicial expression, and alludes to the custom of a judge's rising from his seat when he is going to pronounce sentence. Job was accused by his friends as having led a most wicked life. God will arise, he says, from his judgment seat, and pronounce the sentence *not guilty*. The idea of the whole verse is, that Job, who in the preceding (22) verse, addresses his friends with the words: "Why do you persecute me?" says here: "You may persecute me, you may accuse me that I am wicked, but I know that my avenger liveth, and that at last, *i.e.*, at some future period, and *before my death*, God will stand up in defence of this dust, *i.e.*, this body, and acquit me.

26. And though disease hath destroyed my skin,
     Yet from my flesh I shall see the judge,
27. Whom I shall see on my side,
    And mine eyes shall behold, but not as opponent;
    My heart panteth within me!
28. Then shall ye say: "Why did we persecute him?"
    When the root of the matter is found in me!

26.—This verse has given not less perplexity than the preceding one. The chief difficulty is to *what* or to *whom* does the verb "nokfu" refer? I have followed Good, who joins the *vau* formative of the third person of the verb to "Zoth," which in Arabic signfies " disease, pest, malady." Endless are the conjectures, renderings, and explanations. By my rendering every difficulty is removed; it gives an apposite and clear sense, without any supplemental words.—*Yet from my flesh.*— Whilst being alive. Disease might carry its fearful ravages through all his frame, yet he had the hope of being permitted to see God, his judge, appearing as his avenger before his death.

27.—*Whom shall I see on my side?*—Whose favour I shall experience.—*Panteth.*—His heart panted for that day when God would appear as his avenger.

Having now explained the *words* and *phrases* of these verses, the impartial reader will be sufficiently convinced that there is no reference here whatever to the founder of the Christian faith, neither to the resurrection; in fact, the theory of the resurrection is inconsistent with several passages in this book, where Job expresses a contrary belief. Ch. vii., v. 9: "As the cloud is consumed and vanisheth away, so he that descendeth to hades shall not descend." Ch. x., v. 21: "Before I go, and shall no more return, to the land of darkness and death-shade." Ch. xiv., v. 7, 10, 12: "For there is hope of a tree if it be cut down that it will sprout again, and that its tender branch will not fail; but man dieth and wasteth away, yea, man expireth—and where is he? The waters from the lake fail, and the torrent is diminished and dried up: so man lieth down and riseth not—till the heavens be no more they shall not awake, nor be roused out of their sleep." Ch. xvi., v. 22: "For my few days are come to an end, and I am going the way, whence I shall not return." Surely this is scarcely the language of one believing in the resurrection. It is quite evident that the passage refers to the event recorded in the close of the book. God appeared in the manner corresponding to the meaning of the words of the original. He *came* as the "goël," the avenger of Job, rebuking his friends, and returning him again to prosperity.

28.—*When the root.*—When I am found guiltless. Several Heb. MSS., as also the ancient versions, read: "Bo," *in him,* instead of "Be," *in me.* The sense evidently requires such a reading. We should then render: "Then shall ye say: 'Why did we persecute him, hath any ground of charge been found in him?'"

29. O, tremble ye before the sword!
　　For wrathful is the sword of iniquities;
　　Beware therefore of its judgment!

CHAPTER XX.

1. Then Zophar the Naamathite answered, and said:
2. Truly my thoughts urge me to reply;
　　Wherefore I make haste to do it.
3. I have heard correction reproachful to me,
　　And my discerning spirit causeth me to answer.
4. Knowest thou not this from the most ancient times,
　　From the time that man was placed upon the earth,
5. That the rejoicing of the wicked is short,
　　And the joy of the impious but for a moment?
6. Though his greatness mount up to heaven,
　　And his head reach unto the clouds;
7. Yet he shall perish for ever as the vilest substance;
　　They who saw him shall say: "Where is he?"
8. He shall fly away as a dream, and not be found;
　　Yea, he shall vanish away as a vision in the night;

29.—*Tremble ye before the sword.*—Of the wrath of God.

2.—*Truly my thoughts.*—Translators vary greatly. Vulg.: "Therefore my various thoughts follow on in succession, and the mind is distracted." Sept.: "I did not suppose that thou wouldst speak against these things, and you do not understand more than I." (How this could be made out of the Hebrew I do not know.) Good: "Wither would my tumult transport me, and how far my agitation within me?"

3.—*I have heard.*—He refers to Job's concluding words in the last chapter.—*My discerning spirit.*—Literally: "The spirit of my understanding;" but this idiomatical phrase denotes only "my discerning spirit," or the faculty of understanding.

4.—His purpose is to show that it was the settled arrangement of Providence that the wicked would be overtaken with signal calamity. It was so settled that Job ought not to be surprised that it had occurred in *his* case.—*Placed upon the earth.*—Since the creation.

6.—Sept.: "Though his gifts should go up to heaven, and his sacrifice should touch the clouds." The idea is good, but it is no translation from the Hebrew.

7.—Schultens, Dathe, and Good render: "Amidst his exultation he shall perish for ever."

9. The eye also which saw him, shall see him no more,
   Nor shall his place again behold him;
10. His children shall wander about as beggars;
    For his own hands must restore his wealth;
11. The strength of his youth which filled his bones,
    Shall lie down with him in the dust;
12. Though wickedness be sweet in his mouth,
    Though he hide it under his tongue;
13. Though he retain it, and will not part with it,
    Though he keep it still within his mouth,
14. His food shall be changed within him;
    It shall become the gall of asps within him;
15. The wealth he hath glutted he shall vomit up;
    God shall eject it from him;
16. The poison of asps he shall suck;
    The viper's tongue destroyeth him;

9.—This is almost exactly the same language which Job uses respecting himself. See ch. vii., v. 8, 10.

10.—I have followed Tyndal, Stock, Good, and Wolfsohn. Durell: "The poor shall oppress his children."—*For his own hands.*—So Wolfsohn, and this rendering is in conformity with the original. This clause is variously interpreted. Rosenmüller supposes it means: "And their hands shall restore his iniquity"; that is, what their father took unjustly away.

11.—*The strength of his youth.*—So Rashi, and the Targum. The idea is that he will die in full health and vigour. The translators of the A. V. have followed the Vulg.—Syr. and Arab.: "His bones are full of marrow." Good and several German critics understand by "Alumov," *secret vices*. The former renders: "His secret lusts shall follow his bones; yea, they shall press upon him in the dust."

12.—The idea of this and the following verses is, that though he may have pleasure in indulgence in sin, yet the consequences will be bitter, as if the food which he ate should become like gall.

14.—*Asps.*—The bite of the asp was deadly, and was regarded as incurable. The sight became immediately dim after the bite—a swelling took place, and pain was felt in the stomach, followed by stupor, convulsions, and death. It is probably the same as the *boetan* of the Arabians. It is about a foot in length, and two inches in circumference, its colour being black and white.

16.—*He shall suck.*—The consequences shall be as if he had sucked the poison of asps. It would seem that the ancients regarded the poison of the serpent as deadly, however it was taken into the system. They seem not to have been aware that the poison of a wound may be sucked out without injury to him who does it; and that it is necessary that

17. He shall not see the streamlets of rivers--
The streams of the valleys—of honey and butter;
18. The fruits of his labour he shall return, and not swallow down;
As a possession to be restored in which one rejoiceth not.
19. Because he hath oppressed and forsaken the poor;
Seized a house which he did not build;
20. Because he knew no bound to his appetite;
Because his avarice was insatiable;
21. Because nothing could escape his rapacity:
Therefore his prosperity shall not endure;
22. In the fulness of his abundance he shall be in fear,
Lest misery come upon him from every side;
23. When about to fill himself,
God shall cast on him the fury of His wrath,
And rain it upon him while he is eating;

the poison should mingle with the blood to be fatal.—*Viper's tongue.* —Capt. Riley, in his "Authentic Narrative" (New York, 1817), describes the viper as the "most beautiful object of Nature"; he says that the poison is so virulent as to cause death in 15 minutes.

17.—In our northern regions we have scarcely an idea of butter so liquid as described in this verse; it appears among us in a more solid form. But as the plentiful flowing of honey, when pressed from the comb, may be compared to a little river, as it runs into the vessels in which it is to be kept, so, as they manage matters, butter is equally fluid, and may be described in the same way. A great quantity of butter is made in Barbary, which, after it is boiled with salt, they put into jars, and preserve for use. See Shaw's Travels, p. 169.—Rivers, honey, milk, and butter, are oriental images of earthly felicity.

18.—The idea is that all that he has is like property which a man has, but belongs to another, and is soon to be given up; in such property a man does not find that pleasure which he does n that which he feels to be his own. The Syr. and Arab. have a different reading: "He shall return to labour, but shall not eat; he shall toil, and not be permitted to enjoy the fruit of his labour." Good considers "Yaalos" and "Kecheyl" as pure Arabic words, and renders: "To labour shall he return, but he shall not eat; a dearth his recompense: yea, nothing shall he taste." Houbigant: "He shall restore what he gained by labour, nor shall he consume it; his merchandise were abundant, but he shall not enjoy them."

20.—The Bishop of Killala renders: "Because he acknowledged not the *quail* in his stomach." He seems to have read "Selav," *quail*, as referring to Numb. xi, v. 31, 35. For this allusion *to the quails* he has been much ridiculed.

23.—The idea is that in the midst of his enjoyments God would pour upon him the tokens of his displeasure.

24. Should he flee from the iron weapon,
   The bow of brass shall pierce him through;
25. It is drawn and cometh out of the body,
   The glittering arrow from his gall—
   Terrors are upon him!
26. Every kind of darkness is treasured up for him;
   A fire not blown shall consume him;
   What remaineth in his tent shall perish;
27. The heavens shall reveal his iniquity,
   And the earth riseth up against him;
28. The substance of his house shall roll away
   As the torrents, in the day of His wrath.
29. This is the portion of the wicked man from God,
   And the inheritance appointed to him by the Almighty!

CHAPTER XXI.

1. Then Job answered, and said:
2. Hearken attentively to my speech,
   And let this be your consolation.
3. Suffer me that I may speak,
   And after I have spoken, mock on!
4. Alas for me! Is it not with a man that I speak?
   And if so, why should not my spirit be distressed?

26.—*Darkness.*—Every kind of calamity.—*A fire not blown.*—Rather, "A fire that requires no blowing." It shall be fierce enough without.

27, 28.—Scott remarks that these two verses should be transposed after v. 21, as making a better connection.

2—*Consolation.*—The verb. "nacham" signifies not only *to comfort*, but also *to change one's mind, to repent*; hence we might as well render: "And let this be your retractation" *i.e.*, "Let what I am about to say induce you to *retract* what you have said." Schultens: "And this shall be *in return for* your consolations;" understanding it as spoken ironically. Perhaps the meaning is as Bishop Patrick and Rosenmüller understand it: "All the comfort or consolation that I expect from you, is to hear me."

3.—*Suffer me.*—Allow me to speak without interruption.—*Mock on.* —They might mock his woes, and torture his feelings as they had done, if they would only allow him to express his sentiments.

4.—*Alas for me.*—Job says "I do not reply against God, only to *man*, why then may I not have the privilege of complaining to creatures like myself." Translators and expositors differ greatly.

5. Look on me, and be astonished ;
 And lay your hand upon your mouth.
6. When I think on it, I am confounded,
 And trembling taketh hold of my flesh.
7. Wherefore do the wicked live ;
 Grow old ; yea become mighty in wealth?
8. Their seed is established before them,
 And their offspring in their sight ;
9. Their houses are peaceful, without fear,
 Neither is the rod of God upon them ;
10. Their bull gendereth, and faileth not ;
 Their cow calveth, and casteth not her calf ;
11. They send forth their little ones like a flock,
 And their children skip about ;
12. They sing to the timbrel and harp ;
 They rejoice at the sound of the pipe ;

5.—*Look on me.*—Compare the state in which I was *once*, with that in which I am *now*, and be astonished at the dispensations of God.—*Lay your hand.*—As a token of silence and astonishment. The Egyptian god *Harpocrates*, who was *the god of silence*, is represented with his finger compressing his upper lip.

6.—*When I think on it.*—When I recall the scenes through which I have passed, I feel a shuddering through my body.

7.—*Wherefore.*—You assert that the wicked are punished in this life, how is it then that many wicked live happily and die in peace without any evidence whatever as to God's displeasure ?

8.—You maintained that the children of the wicked are cut off, is it not quite the reverse ? Do we not see that their children grow up, and are established in the presence of their wicked parents ? The word "immom" seems to be an early interpolation, for this word is clearly superfluous.

9.—You maintained that the wicked would never be free from alarm, (see xv., v. 11, 24 ; xx., v. 27, 28) do we not see the contrary ? —*Rod.*—An emblem of punishment.

10.—The idea is that the *wicked* prosper as well as the *pious*.

11.—*Like a flock.*—In great numbers. A beautiful image of prosperity.

12.—*They sing.*—"Yisu," they raise up *their voice* to accompany the timbrel.

13. They wear out their days in pleasure,
   And in an instant they go down to hades.
14. And they say to God: " Depart from us;
   " We desire not the knowledge of Thy ways;
15. " What is the Almighty that we should serve Him,
   "And what will it profit if we pray to Him?——
16. [You say] " Lo, their good is not in their own " power."——
   (Far from me be the defence of the wicked;)
17. But how oft is the lamp of the wicked put out?
   And how oft cometh destruction upon them?
   How often distributeth He sorrows in His anger?
18. They should be as stubble before the wind,
   And as chaff which the storm carrieth away!
19. [You say] " God layeth up his iniquity for his children."——
   Himself He should requite, and he should feel it;
20. His own eyes should see his destruction!
   He himself should drink of the wrath of the Almighty!
21. For what careth he for his house after him,
   When the number of his months are finished?——

~~~~~~~~~~

13.—*They wear out.*—I have translated according to the *Kethiv.* According to the Masora, this is one of the *eleven* words which are written with a *beth*, and must be read with a *caph.* The Antwerp, Paris, and London polyglots read "yeballu," *they wear out*; the Complutensian polyglot, several Hebrew MSS. of Kennicott, and De Rossi, the Sept., Chaldee, Syriac, and Arabic read "yechallu," *they spend.*—*In an instant.*—Without pain, without lingering sickness.

14.—*And they say.*—Not "therefore" as the A. V. It is not the *result* of their mode of living that they reject God, but a *fact*, that they *do* live, even in this prosperity, in the neglect of God.

15.—*What is the Almighty.*—What claim has He that we should be bound to obey and worship Him.

16.—*In their own power.*—They do not enjoy prosperity, do they? They are soon overwhelmed with calamity, are they? How often have *I* seen it otherwise! How often is it a fact that they continue to enjoy prosperity, and live and die in peace!

17.—*Lamp.*—An emblem of *prosperity* and *posterity.*

21.—*What careth he.*—Whatever may happen to his posterity, he does not care.

22. But who shall impart knowledge to God,
   To Him, who judgeth the highest?——
23. One dieth in his full strength,
   Being wholly at ease and quiet;
24. His milk-pails are full of milk,
   And his bones are moistened with marrow;
25. Another dieth in the bitterness of his soul,
   Who never ate with pleasure;
26. Yet they lie down alike in the dust,
   And the worm covereth both.·——
27. Lo! I know your thoughts,
   And the devices by which you would oppress me;
28. For ye say: " Where is the house of the tyrant,
   " And where the dwelling-tents of the wicked ?"
29. Ask then those travellers,
   Whose evidence ye do not doubt ;
30. [They will say] " The wicked is withdrawn in the day of destruction,
   " And is led away in the day of wrath;
31. " Who will charge him with his way to his face,
   " And who repay him what he hath done?
32. " He is borne to the grave,
   " And watch is kept over his tomb;

22.—*Who shall impart.*—This Job says ironically. Perhaps Pope had this passage in view when he wrote :
  "Snatch from his hand the balance and the rod,
  " Rejudge his justice, be the god of God."
The highest.—The great affairs of the Universe.

23.—In this and the following verses Job shows that the inequality of fortune, health, and strength, decides nothing with reference to the *approbation* or *disapprobation* of God. One has a *sudden*, another a *lingering* death, but by none of these can their eternal states be determined.

24.—*His milk pails.*—The word "Atinov" occurs nowhere else, hence all translators differ. Aben Ezra explains it of the places where camels lie down to drink, and Schultens says the same. Good : " His sleek-skin." Wemyss : " The stations of his cattle." Noyes : " His sides." Professor Lee : " His bottles." Syriac : "His sides." Vulg : " His viscera are full of fat." Luther and Wolfsohn : " Milk-pail." Heath : " His granges."

26.—*Lie down alike.*—Death levels all distinction.

30.—*Is withdrawn.*— He is not punished. The translators of the A. V. misunderstood this verse.

33. " Sweet to him are the clods of the valley,
 " And he will draw every man after him,
 " As there were innumerable before him."
34. How then can ye comfort me with vain things,
 Since in your replies there remaineth falsehood?——

PART 4.

CHAPTER XXII.

1. Then Eliphaz the Temanite answered, and said :
2. Can a man be profitable to God,
 As a wise man is profitable to himself?
3. Is it a pleasure to the Almighty that thou art just?
 Or gain to Him that thou makest thy ways perfect?
4. Through fear of thee, will He plead with thee—
 With thee will He enter into judgment?—
5. Is not thy wickedness great?
 And are not thine iniquities innumerable?
6. For of thy brother thou hast taken a pledge for naught,
 And stripped off the clothing of the destitute;
7. To the weary thou hast given no water to drink;
 And hast withholden bread from the hungry;

33.—*And he will draw.*—Some commentators understand this clause as describing an immense funeral procession, in which the dead body was both preceded and followed to the grave by innumerable crowds.

34.—*How then.*—How can you be qualified to give me consolation in my trials, who have such erroneous views of the dealings of God?

2.—*Can a man.*—Can a man confer any favour on God, so as to lay Him under obligation.

4.—*Through fear.*—Job had often expressed a desire to carry his cause before God, and that God would meet him as an equal, and not take advantage of his majesty and power to overwhelm him. So Eliphaz here asks whether God could be expected to meet a *man* in this manner.— *With thee.*—A man whose wickedness is so great.

6.—Good renders conditionally, thus softening the charges brought against Job — *The destitute.*—Literally, *the naked.* A person who was ill-clad, or in rags, was said to be " naked;" as Seneca tells us, Benef. lib. v. 13.

7.—*Given no water.*— It was esteemed a great virtue in the East, to furnish thirsty travellers with water.

8. (As if the land belonged to the man of power alone;
   As if only the man of rank may dwell therein.)
9. Thou hast sent widows away empty,
   And the arms of the fatherless thou hast broken ;
10. Therefore snares are round about thee,
    And sudden fear troubleth thee ;
11. Or darkness, that thou canst not see ;
    Or floods of water cover thee.
12. Is not God in the heights of heaven,
    And looketh on the highest stars, however high they are?
13. Hence thou sayest: "How can God know?
    "Can He judge through the dark cloud?
14. "Thick clouds cover Him that He cannot see ;
    "He walketh only in the circuit of heaven!"
15. Thou indeed keepest to the old way,
    Which wicked men have trodden ;
16. Who were untimely cut down ;
    Whose foundation a flood swept away ;
17. Who said to God : "Depart from us!"
    And : "What could the Almighty do for them?"
18. Yet He filled their houses with good things !
    (But far from me be the defence of the wicked.)

9.—*Thou hast sent.*—Thou hast not done anything to mitigate their sorrows.—*The arms.*—Thou hast taken away all that they relied on. The oppression of the widow and the fatherless was always considered a great crime.

10.—*Snares.*—Sudden calamity.

11.—*Or darkness.*—The sense of this passage in the connection that the particle "or" gives it with the preceding verse is not easy to be ascertained. Houbigant corrects the text and reads : "choshech lo or tireh," *darkness, not light, shalt thou see.*

12.—*Is not.*—Is it not true that because God is so high in heaven, that thou therefore sayest : "What can He do," &c.

14.—*He walketh only.*—He looks not through the mist and darkness that are interposed between earth and heaven, neither does he care for the inhabitants of this world.

16.—*Untimely.*—Prematurely.

17.—*For them.*—The Sept., Syr., and Arab. read "lanu," *for us.* This reading the sense requires.

18.—*Yet he filled.*—The whole verse is a biting sarcasm.—*But far from me.*—He quotes sarcastically Job's words, (xxi., v. 16.)

19. The righteous see it and rejoice,
    And the innocent laugh them to scorn, [saying :]
20. "Truly our adversary is destroyed,
    "And fire hath consumed his abundance!"—
21. Make Him now thy friend, and be at peace;
    Thereby thine increase will be good;
22. Receive, I pray, instruction from His mouth,
    And lay up His words in thine heart.
23. But if thou wilt return to the Almighty, if thou wilt be built up;
    Put then away iniquity far from thy tents;
24. And cast to the dust thy precious treasure,
    And to the stones of the brook the gold of Ophir;
25. And let the Almighty be thy precious treasure,
    And He be as abundance of silver to thee;
26. Then thou mayest delight in the Almighty,
    And lift up thy face unto God;
27. Thou shalt entreat Him, and He will hear thee,
    And thy vows thou shalt accomplish;
28. Thou shalt make a decree,
    And it shall be established for thee;
    And the light shall shine upon thy ways;
29. When men are cast down, thou shalt say: "Cheer up!
    "For the dejected He will save."

19.—*See it.*—The destruction of the wicked.

20.—*Our adversary.*—I have followed Gesenius. Rosenmüller. and Noyes. Good: "For our tribe is not cut off." Durell: "Is not their standing corn cut down?"

24.—Heath renders: "And count the fine gold as dust, and the gold of Ophir as the stones of the brook." Kimchi, and after him Grotius, supposes that it means: "Thy gold thou shalt regard no more than dust, and gold of Ophir no more than the stones of the brook; God shall be to thee better than gold and silver." The Sept.: "Thou shalt be placed on a mount in a rock, and as a rock on the torrent of Ophir." Vulg.: "He shall give for earth flint, and for flint golden torrents.

26.— *Lift up thy face.*—An emblem of prosperity, happiness, and conscious innocence.

28.—*Make a decree.*—Form a purpose or plan, and it shall not be frustrated.

29, 30.—There is great difficulty in these two verses, and all the translations vary. I confess that the real meaning of the two verses

30. He will deliver even him who is not innocent;
He will be delivered by the purity of thy hands.

CHAPTER XXIII.

1. Then Job answered, and said:
2. Is my complaint still rebellion?
Is not the hand that is upon me heavier than my groaning?
3. O that I knew where I might find Him!
I would come to His tribunal;
4. I would order my cause before Him,
And fill my mouth with arguments;
5. I would know the answers He would make to me,
And understand what He would say to me;
6. Would He plead against me with His great power?
No;—Surely He would concede unto me.
7. There the righteous man might argue with Him,
And I should triumphantly be acquitted by my judge.

I do not understand. The rendering in the A. V. of verse 30, "He shall deliver *the island* of the innocent," is a very unhappy one, and the translators had, it would seem, no idea of the meaning of the passage.

2.—*Is my complaint still rebellion.*—Do you construe my lamentations over my unparalleled suffering as rebellion against God.—"Meri," root "Marah," *he rebelled.*—*The hand.*—Is not the calamity inflicted upon me, heavier than my complaint? The Sept., Syr., and Arab. read "yado," *his* hand.

3.—*O that I knew.*—The argument had been with his three friends, and he saw that there was no use in attempting further to convince them. If he could get the cause before God, and be allowed to plead it there, he felt assured that justice would be done him.

4.—*Order my cause.*—I would arrange my arguments, or plead my cause, as one does in a court of justice.—*Fill my mouth with arguments.*—I would appeal to the evidence furnished by a life of benevolence and justice, that I am not a hypocrite.

5.—*The answer he would make.*—What His decision in my case would be.

6.—*With His great power.*—Would he take advantage of his *power* to triumph over me?—*Concede.*—This is the sense of the verb.

7.—*The righteous.*—Though Job speaks here in the *third* person, he no doubt refers to himself.—*Triumphantly.*—This is the meaning of the original as well as "for ever," and suits the connection better.

8. But, behold, I go to the East, and He is not there;
And to the West, but I cannot perceive Him;
9. To the North where He worketh, yet I behold Him not;
He hideth Himself in the South, that I cannot see Him;
10. But He knoweth the way which I take;
When He hath tried me, I shall come forth as gold;
11. In His steps I have fixed my foot;
His way I have kept, and not turned aside;
12. From the commandment of His lips I departed not;
In my bosom I have stored up the words of His mouth;——
13. But He is One, and who can dissuade Him?
For what He desireth that He doeth.
14. Therefore He performeth what is appointed for me;
And how many such things may yet be with Him!
15. Therefore I am troubled at His presence;
When I consider, I am afraid of Him;

8.—*To the East.*—In the rendering of these verses I have followed Rashi and the Targum. Oriental geographers considered themselves as facing the East; hence the West behind them, the South on the right hand, and the North on the left.

9.—*Where he worketh.*—Rashi: "When He *created* (the North,) He did not put His throne there, that I might see Him there." The passage in the original is rather difficult.—*Hideth Himself.*—The Southern regions, on account of the impossibility of passing through the heat of the torrid zone, were supposed to be inaccessible. To those hidden and unknown quarters Job says, he turned to see if God was there to be found.

10.—*The way which I take.*—He approves of my conduct.—*As gold.*—Pure as gold purified from all alloy.

11.—*Fixed my foot.*—I have adhered tenaciously to Him.

12.—*In my bosom.*—So Good; and though not according to the Masoretic points, this sense is more agreeable to the context than "necessary food."

13.—*He is One.*—From the Unity of God Job rightly infers that His power and dominion are absolute; that the dispensations of His providence are not to be controlled.

14.—*Therefore*—All the calamities He has reserved for me will come upon me, and who knows what his intention yet is with me, what more punishment He has in store for me.

15.—*When I consider.*—When I think closely on the dealings of God.

16. For God hath made my heart soft,
   And the Almighty hath troubled me;
17. O why was I not cut off before the darkness?
   Why hath He covered the darkness from me?

XXIV.
1. Why, since no events are hidden from the Almighty,
   Do not His friends perceive His days?
2. Here, they remove the landmarks;
   They drive off the flocks and feed thereon;
3. The ass of the orphan they drive away;
   They take the widow's ox for a pledge;
4. They turn the needy out of the way;
   The poor of the land must hide themselves together;
5. Behold as wild asses in the desert,
   They go forth to their work,
   Rising early for the pillage of the wilderness,
   The bread of themselves and of their children.——
6. In the field they reap his corn;
   And crop the oppressor's vineyard;
7. Naked they lodge without clothing,
   Without covering from the cold;

16.—*Soft.*—He has deprived me of fortitude and courage.

17.—*Before the darkness.*—Before these calamities came upon me. —*Covered the darkness.*—Job means that he was not permitted to see death, and he complains that God denied him the only refuge from his sorrows—a grave. See Scott and Rosenmüller.

1.—Job asks: "Why does God, who knows the conduct of men, not come forth to deal with men according to their true character?" Good: "Wherefore are not doomdays kept by the Almighty, so that His offenders may eye His periods?" Noyes: "Why are not times of punishment reserved by the Almighty, and why do not they who regard Him see His judgments?" The Targum renders "ittim" *iddanaya, set times.*—*His days.*—When He punishes the wicked.

2.—*Feed thereon.*—Good renders "yiru," *they destroy*, deriving the word, not from "raah," *to feed*, but from "rá," *to rend, to destroy.*

4.—*They turn.*—They do not allow them the advantages of the highway.—*Must hide.*—For fear of the rich and the mighty.

6.—The Targum: "They reap in a field that is not their own." Vulg., Sept., and Kimchi the same. They evidently divided the Hebrew word "belilo" in two, though De Rossi observes that none of the MSS. collated read the word in *two.*

7.—*They lodge.*—Another characteristic of the wandering Arabs. They are *ill-fed, ill-clothed*, and often even *without tents*. They are plunderers, and are often obliged to fly for their lives, and cannot encumber themselves with what is not absolutely needful.

8. Drenched are they with mountain showers,
   And embrace the rock for lack of shelter!
9. There, they tear away the fatherless from the breast;
   The suckling of the poor they take for a pledge;
10. The naked they cause to go without clothing,
    And famished are those who carry the sheaves.
11. Within dark walls they cause them to press oil;
    They tread wine presses, yet suffer thirst.
12. Here, from the city mortals groan;
    There, the soul of the wounded crieth out;
    Yet no judge regardeth the supplication.——
13. Others hate the light;
    They know not its ways;
    They abide not upon its paths;
14. At early dawn riseth the murderer,
    Poor and needy, he sheddeth blood;
    In the night he is a thief,
15. Waiting, as the eye of the adulterer, for the twilight,
    Saying: "No eye will see me;"
    And putteth a mask upon his face;

8.—*Embrace the rock.*—Niebuhr, speaking of the wandering Arabs near Mount Sinai, says: "Those who cannot afford a tent, spread out a cloth upon four or six stakes. Others spread their cloth near a tree, or endeavour to shelter themselves from the heat and the rain in the cavities of the rocks." Reisebeschreib. i. Th., seite 233.

9.—*Tear away.*—They make slaves of them for their own use, or sell them.—*Suckling.*—So Wolfsohn.

10.—*The naked.*—They compel the poor to drudge in the fields in the most violent heats.—*Carry the sheaves.*—Moses commanded that even the ox should not be muzzled that trod out the corn (Deut. xxv., v. 4); still more cruel it would be in compelling men to carry sheaves, without allowing them even to satisfy their hunger.

11.—*Dark walls.*—Refusing them oil in the lamp, whilst they were pressing oil.—*They tread.*—Compel them to tread out their grapes, without allowing them to slake their thirst from the wine.

12.—*Supplication.*—Several Hebrew MSS. read "tefillah," not "tiflah."

14.—*Poor and needy.*—I consider both nouns in the *nominative*, not in the *objective* case. His object is plunder, and he could not expect success by slaying the poor.

16. And diggeth in the dark through houses;
In the daytime they shut themselves up;
They know not the light;
17. For the morning to them is as death-shade;
For they are familiar with the terrors of death-shade:
18. Miserable should he be on the waters;
His part in the land should be accursed;
He should not walk in the path of the nobles!
19. As drought and heat consume the snow-waters,
So should hades those who have sinned;
20. The womb should forget him;
The worm should sweetly feed on him;
He should be no more remembered;
So iniquity should be broken as a tree.——
21. One nourisheth the barren, who beareth not;
But to the widow he doeth not good;
22. The mighty also he destroyeth by his power;
He riseth up, and no one is sure of life!
23. To such He giveth safety, and they are sustained;
Though His eyes are on their ways.

16.—*And diggeth.*—"In Bengal it is common for thieves to dig through the walls of houses made of mud, or under the house floors, which are made merely of earth, and enter thus into the dwellings while the inmates are asleep." Rosenmüller's "Alte und neue Morgenland" *in loco.*—*They shut themselves up.*—So Kimchi. The rendering of the A. V. is contrary to the general sense of the passage.

18.—There is scarcely a passage in the book more obscure than this, and the variety of renderings shows the perplexity of expositors. In my opinion, Job describes here (v. 18-20) *how* such sinners should be treated, and intimates that they are not *so* treated, as appears from common observation. All the verbs are in the future, and I think ought to be rendered in the conditional mood. Thus rendered, they are agreeable to the opinions which Job constantly maintained.

20,—*The womb.*—The mother that bare him should forget him.—*The worm.*—The Targum: "The cruel, who have neglected to commiserate the poor, shall be sweet to the worms."

21.—*Nourisheth.*—See Rashi's comment on this passage.

23.—*He giveth.*—It is usual for this writer abruptly to introduce the Almighty, without mentioning his name.—*Though His eyes.*—Though He sees their wicked deeds.

24. They are exalted for a while—and are not;
 They are cut off as the ears of corn;
 Are laid low, and, like all, shut up in the tomb.
25. If it be not so, who will confute me,
 And make my speech worthless?

CHAPTER XXV.

1. Then Bildad the Shuhite answered, and said:
2. Dominion and terror are with Him;
 He worketh absolutely in His high places.
3. Is there any numbering of His troops?
 And upon whom doth not His light arise?
4. How then can man be just before God?
 And how can he—born of a woman—be clean?
5. Behold even the moon, and it shineth not;
 Yea, the stars are not bright in His sight;

24.—Job complains, *first*, that they are exalted; *secondly*, that they die an easy death in mature age, cut off as the ears of ripe corn; *thirdly*, that they have an honourable interment. Like men in general, they are shut up in the tomb, when, for their wickedness, they ought to have been left as a prey to wild beasts.

25.—Job here challenges any one to prove the contrary to what he had said.

1.—It is most remarkable that Bildad here does not attempt to meet the appeals which Job had made to facts, or reply to his arguments. All that he does is only to *repeat* what had been said before. And more striking still is the omission of the *third* reply of Zophar. Again, the *eleven* verses which conclude the 27th chapter, and are now given as the words of *Job*, cannot have been spoken by Job; because they contain such doctrine as Job himself could not hold, and which indeed he expressly denies, namely, that *great calamities prove great wickedness*. I would therefore propose the following changes in the division of the speeches from chapter xxv. to xxviii.—

Reply of Bildad:—
 Ch. xxv., v. 1 to 6.
 Ch. xxvi., v. 5 to the end of the chapter.
Reply of Job:—
 Ch. xxvi., v. 1 to 4 inclusive.
 Ch. xxvii., v. 2 to 12 inclusive.
Reply of Zophar:
 Ch. xxvii., v. 13, until the end of chapter xxviii.

3.—*His troops.*—See Daniel, ch., iv. v. 35.,
4.—See ch. iv., v. 17, 18; ch. xv., v. 15, 16.
5.—In comparison with God, the moon is dark and obscure. The Targum: "Behold the moon is as yet spotted in her eastern part; the sun shineth not, and the stars are not pure in His sight."

6. How much less man, who is but corruption;
   The son of man, who is only a worm?——

CHAPTER XXVI.

1. Then Job answered, and said:
2. How hast thou helped the powerless,
   And strengthened the feeble arm!
3. How hast thou counselled the ignorant,
   And made much sound wisdom known!
4. From whom hast thou pillaged these words?
   And whose inspired words came from thee?——

5. The mighty dead, and those dwelling with them,
   Tremble beneath the waters;

6.—The Targum: "How much more man, who in his life is a reptile; and the son of man, who in his death is a worm."

2.—A strong irony, addressed to Bildad, and so the Targumist understood these verses. His paraphrase is: "Why hast thou pretended to give succour, when thou art without strength? And save while thine arm is weak? Why hast thou given counsel, when thou art without understanding?" Herder renders this passage as if it related wholly to God: "Whom helpest Thou? Him who hath no strength? Whom dost Thou vindicate? Him whose arm hath no power? To whom give counsel? One without wisdom? Truly, much wisdom hast Thou taught him!"—*Strengthened the feeble arm.*—He had come professedly to comfort and support his afflicted friend in his trials. Yet Job asks, what there was in his observations that were fitted to produce this effect? Instead of declaiming on the majesty and greatness of God, he should have said something that was adapted to relieve an afflicted and troubled soul.

3.—*Much sound wisdom.*—Heath: "Verily, thou hast been teaching learning to the Master." Good: "How hast thou made known the matter in debate?"

5.—This is a continuation of the reply of Bildad, and ought to follow after the end of the last verse of chapter xxv. See note xxv., v. 1. This verse, as rendered in the A. V., conveys no meaning: the Hebrew is rather obscure. The word "rephaim" is rendered by the Sept., Vulg., Chaldee, Arab., and Syr. by "giants;" but by their rendering the true meaning of the passage cannot be determined. Rashi: "Gehenna." *I* cannot understand why the author gives the place of the departed *under the waters.*

6. Hades is naked before Him,
    And destruction hath no covering;
7. He stretcheth out the North over empty space,
    And hangeth the earth upon nothing;
8. He bindeth up the waters in His thick clouds,
    Yet the cloud is not rent beneath them;
9. He withdraweth the face of His throne,
    Overspreading it with His cloud;
10. He decreed a boundary to the waters
    Until the end of the light and the darkness;

6.—*Hades.*—The rendering "hell" is misleading, for it does not mean *a place of punishment*, but the place where all the dead are supposed to be gathered together.—*Is naked.*—He sees all its inhabitants, knows all their employments, and sways a sceptre over them all.—*Hath no covering.*—There is nothing to conceal it from God. There is a passage similar to this in Homer, Iliad xx., 61-66 :

"Deep in the dismal regions of the dead,
Th' infernal monarch reared his horrid head,
Leaped from his throne, lest Neptune's arm should lay
His dark dominions open to the day,
And pour in light on Pluto's drear abodes,
Abhorred by men, and dreadful e'en to gods."—*Pope*.

7.—*Empty space—nothing.*—Without anything to support it. The Targum: "He hangeth the earth *upon the waters*, nothing sustaining it."

8.—The wonder which Bildad here expresses is, that so large a quantity of water as is poured down from the clouds should be held suspended in the air, without seeming to rend the cloud, and falling all at once.

9.—*Withdraweth.*—God is often represented as encompassed with clouds, or as accompanied with tempests.—*Overspreading it.*—The clouds are made to conceal the splendour of the throne of God from the sight of man.

10.—*A boundary.*—The powerful law which God gave to the sea keeps it within those precincts as exactly as if a circle had been drawn around it. A similar idea Milton has beautifully expressed in his account of the creation :

"Then stayed the fervid wheels, and in his hand
He took the golden compasses, prepared
In God's eternal store, to circumscribe
This universe, and all created things :
One foot he centered, and the other turned
Round through the vast profundity obscure ;
And said : 'Thus far extend thy bounds,
This be thy just circumference, O world!'"—*Per. Lost*, b. vii.

Until the end.—The author turns our thoughts to another operation of Providence—the constant succession of *day* and *night*.

11. The pillars of heaven tremble,
    And are confounded at His rebuke;
12. By His power the sea roareth,
    And by His wisdom He represseth its pride;
13. By His wind He garnisheth the heavens;
    His hand pierceth the shooting serpent;
14. Lo! these are but the outlines of His ways;
    And how faint the whisper which we hear of Him!
    For the thunder of His power who can understand?———

CHAPTER XXVII.

(1. Moreover, Job continued his discourse and said:)
2. As God liveth, who hath neglected my cause,
   And the Almighty who hath distressed my soul,

11.—*Pillars of heaven.*—Perhaps an allusion is here made to the *high mountains*, which were anciently esteemed by the common people as the *pillars* on which the *heavens* rested; and when these were shaken with earthquakes it might be said "the pillars of heaven tremble." Mount *Atlas* was supposed to be one of those pillars, and this gave rise to the fable of Atlas being a man who bore the heavens on his shoulders.

12.—*The sea roareth.*—Vulg. and Rashi: "By His power the waters of the sea are congregated together." Luther: "The sea becomes suddenly tempesteous." Noyes: "He stilleth the sea;" as though it had a reference to the dividing of the sea when the Israelites left Egypt. Herder: "By His power He scourgeth the sea, by His wisdom He bindeth its pride."

13.—*By His wind.*—The beauty of a clear and serene sky is meant here.—*Shooting serpent.*—See Isa. xxvii., v. 1. By the *shooting serpent*, the Arabic writers understand the stars called the *Dragon*, which lie between the Ursa Major and Minor, near the North Pole. This is probably the same constellation described by Virgil:

> Around our pole the spiry Dragon glides,
> And, like a winding stream, the Bears divides;
> The less and greater, who by Fate's decree
> Abhor to die beneath the southern sea.—*Dryden.*

14.—*The thunder.*—If, when God speaks in such faint and gentle tones, we are so much impressed with a sense of His greatness and glory, who would not be overwhelmed if He were to speak out as in thunder? Thus ends the reply of Bildad. He did not attempt to reply to any of the arguments of Job. It seems that he did not know how to meet the line of argument which Job had pursued.

2.—This is a continuation of ch. xxvi., v. 4. Job says that such was his confidence in his own sincerity and truth, that he could make his appeal to God, even though he knew that He had hitherto treated

3. As long as I have life in me,
   And the breath of God is in my nostrils;
4. My lips shall not speak wickedness,
   Nor my tongue utter deceit!
5. Far be it therefore from me that I should justify you;
   Till I expire I will not relinquish my integrity!
6. My righteousness I hold fast, and will not let it go;
   Nor shall my heart reproach me while I live!
7. (May mine enemy be as the wicked,
   And mine adversary as the unjust.)
8. For what is the hope of the impious,
   Though he hath amassed wealth,
   When God taketh away his life?
9. Will God then attend to his cry,
   When trouble cometh upon him?
10. Did he delight himself in the Almighty?
    Did he always call upon God?———
11. Shall I teach you the dealings of God?
    Not conceal what is with the Almighty?
12. Behold, ye yourselves have indeed all seen it;
    Why then do ye cherish such vain opinions?———

---

him as if he were guilty.—*As God liveth.*—A form of solemn adjuration, or an oath by the living God. It is the form by which God often swears. See Ezek. xiv., v. 16; xxxiii., v. 11.

3.—*Breath of God.*—The breath which God breathed into man when He created him. Gen. ch. ii., v. 7.

4.—*My lips.*—This is a solemn assurance that he did not mean to vindicate the cause of wickedness.—*Utter deceit.*—No consideration should ever induce him to countenance error or to palliate wrong.

5.—*Far be it.*—I will not part with my claim to the character of an honest man, by giving my sanction to your principles and opinions.

6.—*Reproach me.*—As being insincere or false. Good contends that the verb is here in Niphal: "My heart shall not *be reproached.*"

7.—He refers to his friends, with whom he had been disputing.

8.—The same sentiment had before been expressed by Bildad (ch. viii.), and by Zophar (ch. xx.) Job says that he fully accords with that belief, and that he had no sympathy for impiety. The Targum: "What can the detractor expect who hath amassed the mammon of unrighteousness when God taketh away his life?"

11.—*The dealings.*—Targum: "By the prophecy of God."

12.—*Behold.*—Your own experience and observation have shown you that the righteous are frequently in affliction, and the wicked in affluence. Here ends the reply of Job.

13. This is the portion of a wicked man from God;
   The inheritance which oppressors receive from the Almighty;
14. If his children be multiplied, it is for the sword;
   And his offspring shall not be satisfied with bread;
15. His posterity shall be buried by Death,
   And his widows shall not weep;
16. Though he heap up silver as dust,
   And prepare raiment as the mire,
17. He may prepare it, but the just shall wear it;
   And the innocent shall share the silver;
18. He buildeth his house like the moth-worm,
   Or like a shed which the watchman maketh;
19. He may lie down a rich man, and nothing be taken away;
   He openeth his eyes, and nothing remaineth to him.

13.—Here begins the third reply of Zophar, and we should insert here: "THEN ZOPHAR THE NAAMATHITE ANSWERED AND SAID." The sentiments expressed here accord exactly with what *Zophar* might be expected to advance, and are exactly in his style. See ch. xxv., v. 1 note.—*The inheritance.*—What tyrants must expect to receive from God.

14.—*His offspring.*—The same sentiment Zophar had advanced before. Ch. xx., v. 10.

15.—*By death.*—They shall not be buried at all. This passage has a striking resemblance to Jer. xxii., v. 18, 19. Good, who follows the Targum: "Entombed in corruption."—*Widows.*—A proof that *polygamy* was then practised.

16.—Compare 1 Kings x., v. 27.—*Prepare raiment.*—Oriental wealth consisted much in changes of raiments, and, as fashions never change there, they are valuable until they are worn out. Bokteri, a poet of Cufah, in the ninth century, had so many presents made to him in the course of his life, that when he died he was found possessed of a hundred complete suits of clothes, two hundred shirts, and five hundred turbans; D'Herbelot, page 208. This and the following verse are called "the introverted parallelism;" the *fourth* member answers to the *first*, and the *third* to the *second*.

18.—*Moth-worm.*—Who, by eating the garment which is its habitation, destroys its own dwelling. The Targum renders "spider." This does also well correspond with the idea expressed by Zophar.—*The watchman.*—He who watches the vineyards makes a temporary shelter from the cold at night.

19.—Rich he shall retire to rest in the evening, and poor he shall rise in the morning. Translators and commentators have all misunderstood this verse.

20. Terrors rush upon him like waters;
    In the night a tempest stealeth him away;
21. The east wind carrieth him away, and he departeth,
    And it hurrieth him from his place:
22. It driveth upon him, and doth not spare;
    From its power fain would he escape;
23. It shall clap its hands at him,
    And shall hiss him from his place.

XXVIII.
1. Truly there is a mine for silver,
   And a place for gold which men refine;
2. Iron is taken from the earth,
   And ore is fused into copper;
3. Man delveth into the regions of darkness,
   And examineth to the utmost limit
   The stones of darkness and death-shade;

20.—*Stealeth him away.*—He dieth suddenly.

22-23.—These two verses refer to the east wind or storm, who is here personified. The same sentiment was expressed by Bildad, ch. xviii., v. 18.

1.—*A mine.*—Professor Lee: "There is an outlet for the silver," *i.e.*, the separation of the silver from the earthy particles by which it is surrounded in the ore. Sept.: "There is a place for silver whence it is obtained." The idea is, that man had evinced his wisdom in finding out the mines of silver, and working them.—Gold and silver are mentioned as known in the earliest ages. Pharaoh arrayed Joseph in vestures of fine linen, and put a chain of gold around his neck, Gen. xli., v. 42; and great quantities of gold and silver ornaments were borrowed by the Israelites of the Egyptians, when they were about to go to the promised land. Homer's account of the shield of Achilles (Il. xviii., 474) proves that the art of working in the precious metals was well known in his time. In Egypt, ornaments of gold and silver, consisting of rings, bracelets, necklaces, and trinkets, have been found of the times of Osirtasen I., and Thothmes III. On the early use of the metals among the ancient Egyptians see Wilkinson's "Manners and Customs of the Ancient Egyptians, vol. iii., p. 215.

2.—*Iron.*—Iron was early known; Tubal Cain was instructor in iron and brass; Gen. iv., v. 22.—*Ore.*—The Hebrew word "Eben" (stone) means *ore* in the form of stone.—*Copper.*—Not *brass*, because it is not found in ore.

3.—*Delveth.*—The entire passage to verse 12 refers to the deep skill and ingenuity of man. The passage, however, instead of being applied to *man*, has by most commentators been referred to the Deity; and thus the whole has been completely misunderstood, and what is perfectly clear, been regarded as inextricably perplext and mysterious.

4. They work a shaft from where they sojourn;
   Lo! they forget the use of the foot;
   They descend and wander from men;
5. The earth—out of it cometh forth bread;
   Though its interior is subverted by fire;
6. Yet among its stones is the place of the sapphire,
   And the ore of gold is found in it;
7. The path thereto no bird of prey knoweth;
   Nor hath the eye of the vulture seen it;
8. Wild beasts have not trodden it;
   The fierce lion hath not walked over it;
9. Man layeth his hand upon the flinty rock;
   He overturneth mountains from their foundations;
10. He cutteth channels among the rocks,
    And his eye seeth every precious thing;

4.—*They work a shaft.*—The connexion naturally suggests, that this ambiguous text refers to the art of mining, and of obtaining metals.—*They forget.*—He refers not only to the manner in which they descend into pits, but also to the manner in which they dig the ore. The shaft or passage being low, they work sometimes on their *knees*, and often sitting, so that they make little use of their feet. Herder:
"A flood goeth out from the realm of oblivion,
They draw it up from the foot of the mountain,
They remove it away from men."
Yet he says: "The passage remains obscure to my mind."
Noyes:
"From the place where they dwell they open a shaft,
Unsupported by the feet,
They are suspended, they swing away from men."

5.—*The earth.*—Here he represents the dangers to which miners are exposed.—*Its interior.*—By the miners it is subverted as if by fire. Good: "The earth of itself poureth forth bread; But below it, windeth a fiery region." Luther: "They bring fire from the earth beneath, when food grows up above."

6.—Here is the temptation to risk the forementioned dangers. The Sapphire is a precious stone, usually of a blue colour, though it is sometimes yellow, red, violet, green, or white. In hardness it is inferior to the diamond only. The sapphire is, next to the diamond, the most valuable of the precious stones.

7-8.—An illustration of man's intrepidity in penetrating these dangerous regions of darkness. The most daring beasts of prey would not venture into them.

9.—*Overturneth.*—Digs under them, and they fall.

11. He restraineth the oozing streams,
    And bringeth hidden things to light;
12. But where shall wisdom be found?
    Yea, where the place of understanding?
13. Man knoweth not the seat thereof;
    Nor can it be found in the land of the living;
14. The abyss saith: "It is not in me;"
    And the sea saith: "It is not in me."
15. Solid gold cannot purchase it;
    Nor silver be weighed out as its price;
16. It cannot be bartered for the ingot of Ophir;
    For the precious onyx, or the sapphire;
17. Gold and the crystal cannot equal it;
    Nor can it be exchanged for jewels of pure gold;
18. Let not RAMOTH and GABISH be mentioned;
    For the price of wisdom is above pearls;
19. The topaz of Cush cannot equal it;
    Nor can it be bartered for pure gold.
20. Whence then cometh this wisdom?
    And where is the place of understanding?

11.—*Restraineth.*—He contrives methods to prevent the waters from impeding his operations.

13.—*The seat thereof.*—So Herder and Wolfsohn. This is no doubt the true rendering, and far better than to render: "Man knoweth not the *price* thereof;" because this forms no proper answer to the question in the previous verse; as the question is *where* wisdom is to be found, *not* what is its *value*. Professor Lee: "Man knoweth not its *equal*." Good: "Man knoweth not its *source*.

14.—The object of this and the following verse is to show that wisdom cannot be found in the deepest recesses to which man can penetrate, nor purchased by anything which man possesses.

15.—*Weighed out.*—Before the art of coining was known, it was common to *weigh* the precious metals that were used as a medium of trade.

16.—*Ingot.*—When gold is refined, it is cast into small bars, and stamped; these are called *ingots*, gold of due value.

17.—*Crystal.*—Jerome, "glass." Sept., "crystal." It is doubtful whether *glass* was known so early as this. Dr. Shaw supposes the *diamond* to be meant.

18.—*Ramoth—Gabish.*—What these words signify I know not; I have therefore not translated them. *Ramoth* also occurs in Ezek. xxvii, v. 16, where it is mentioned as a valuable commodity in merchandise in which Syria traded with Tyre, and occurs in connection with emeralds, purple, broidered work, fine linen, and agate.

21. Since it is hid from the eyes of all living,
And concealed from the birds of the air?
22. DESTRUCTION and DEATH say:
"We have only heard of its fame."
23. God only understandeth its way,
And He only knoweth its place.
24. For He beholdeth the ends of the earth;
What is under the whole heavens He seeth.
25. When to the winds He gave weight,
And measured out the waters;
26. When He made a course for the rain,
And a path for the thunder-flash:
27. Then did He see and declare it,
He searched it out, and established it;
28. And to man He said:
"Lo! the fear of the Lord—that is wisdom;
"And to depart from evil, is understanding."

CHAPTER XXIX.

1. And Job continued his discouse, and said:
2. O that I were as in months past,

21.—*Birds of the air.*—Crinsoz supposes that they may be used figuratively to denote astronomers who, though they can calculate the distances and motions of the stars, cannot find out this wisdom. Rashi: "Angels." Umbreit remarks on this passage, that there is attributed to the fowls in Oriental countries a deep knowledge, and an extraordinary gift of divination, and that they appear as the interpreters and confidants of the Gods.—Comp. Eccles. x., v. 20.

25.—By barometical observations, taken every hour from the latitude of 1 degree north to 1 degree south, it appears that the combined actions of the sun and moon produce a flux and reflux of the atmosphere, causing in the barometer the variation of a line and $\frac{7}{10}$ of the English division, which supposes a rise and fall in the atmosphere of about a hundred feet; while the combined action of the sun and moon, according to Mr. Bernoulli, causes an elevation in the sea at the equator of only seven feet.—Perouse's voyage round the world, vol. ii., pp. 513, 523.

27.—*See.*—Wisdom. See Prov. viii., v. 27-30.

28.—Professor Lee supposes that this refers to the instruction which God gave in Paradise to our first parents.

2.—*O that I were.*—Job designed to show his friends that his lamentations were not unreasonable, when it was borne in mind from what a state of prosperity he had been taken, and to what a condition of woe he had been brought. He dwells particularly upon the good

As in the days when God watched over me!
3. When His lamp shone upon my head;
   When by His light I walked through darkness;
4. As I was in the days of my strength;
   When God took counsel with me in my tent;
5. When the Almighty was yet with me;
   When my servants were round about me;
6. When I washed my steps in cream,
   And the rock poured out for me streams of oil;
7. When I went to the gate through the city;
   When I prepared my seat in the public place:
8. The young men saw me, and retired before me,
   And the aged rose up, and stood;
9. The princes refrained from speaking,
   And laid their hand upon their mouth;
10. The voice of nobles was silent,
    And their tongue cleaved to the roof of their mouth;

which he was enabled then to do, and the respect which was shown him as a public benefactor.

3.—*Shone.*—The Hebrew word "behillo" is, according to Ewald and Gesenius the *hiphil* of "halal," *to shine*; according to Schultens and Rosenmüller it is the *infinitive* of *kal*, with a pleonastic suffix, meaning "when it shined," *i.e.*, the light. The sense is the same.

4.—*Strength.*—The passage shows that it does *not* mean *youth;* for Job describes the respect shown to him when in mature life.—*When God took counsel.*—The idea is that God came into his tent as a friend, and that he was as it were made acquainted with God's plans.

5.—*When the Almighty.*—Good takes "shaddai" in the Arabic sense, and renders: "When my *strength* was yet in me."

6.—*The rock.*—Compare Deut. xxxii., v. 13.

7.—*To the gate.*—The Sept. reads "shachar," *morning*, instead of "shaar," *gate*: "When I went forth *in the morning* to the city."—*Prepared my seat.*—Job here speaks of himself as a civil magistrate—as a judge upon the bench, who had a seat erected for him to sit on, whilst he was hearing and trying causes. This was set up in the street, in the open air, before the gate of the city, where great numbers might be convened, and hear and see justice administered. The Arabs to this day hold their courts of justice in an open place, under the heavens, or in a market place. See Norden's "Travels in Egypt," vol. ii., p. 140.

8.—A beautiful illustration of oriental manners, and of the respect paid to a man of distinction.—*And stood.*—They continued to stand still until I had passed by. See Bishop Lowth's Lect., vol. ii., p. 412.

9.—*Laid their hand.*—See chapter xxi., v. 5 note.

11. When the ear heard, it blessed me;
 When the eye saw, it bore witness to me;
12. For I rescued the poor who cried,
 And the orphan, when there was none to help him;
13. The blessing of the wandering came upon me,
 And the heart of the widow I made glad;
14. I put on righteousness, and it clothed me,
 And justice was my robe and diadem;
15. I was eyes to the blind,
 And feet was I to the lame;
16. I was a father to the poor;
 And the cause of the unknown I searched out;
17. And I broke the grinders of the wicked,
 And plucked the prey from his teeth:———

18. Hence I said : " I shall die in my nest ;
 I shall multiply my days as the Phœnix;
19. My root is spread out to the waters;
 The dew layeth all night on my branches;

11.—*It bore witness.*—The admiration which was shown by the eyes of the multitude was witness of the respect in which I was held.

12.—*I rescued.*—When a poor man, who had no means of employing counsel, brought his cause before me, I delivered him from the hand of his oppressor.

13.—*I made glad.*—By vindicating her cause.

14.—*It clothed me.*— It formed the constant moral habit of my character. This metaphor, derived from the exterior dress, and applied to the qualities and endowments of the mind, is extremely frequent in the language of Scripture. Compare Ps. xciii, v. 1; cxxx., v. 16-18 ; Isa. lix., v. 17.—*And justice.*—His decisions in the court of justice procured him all the honour given to a king, without the regal dress and title.

15.—*I was eyes.*—I was their counsellor and guide.

16.—*Of the unknown.*—As a judge he gave particular attention to the cause of the stranger. So Rosenmüller, Herder, Wolfsohn, and Good.

18-20.—Thesē verses ought to come at the end of the chapter.
—*Die in my nest.*—Schultens justly observes that the image is borrowed from the eagle, who, it is well known, builds her nest on the summit of the highest rocks.—*Phœnix.*—"All animals obeyed the woman in eating the forbidden fruit, except one bird, by the name of "hul."—Bereshith Rabba.

19.—*The dew.*—As a tree standing on the verge of the river, and watered each night by copious dews, appears beautiful and flourishing, so is my condition. Hasselquist, speaking of the excessively hot weather in Egypt says : " The dew is particularly serviceable to the

20. My glory will be fresh in me,
    And my bow renew in my hand;——

21. To me men gave ear and waited,
    And were silent at my counsel;
22. After my words they replied not,
    And my speech dropped upon them;
23. For me they waited as for the rain,
    And opened their mouths as for the harvest-rain;
24. If I smiled on them, they were not confident,
    Nor cast down the light of my countenance;
25. I chose out their way, and sat as chief;
    I dwelt as a king in the midst of an army,
    And as a comforter among mourners;

XXX. 1. But now they who are younger than I
    Hold me in derision,
    Whose fathers I should have disdained
    To rank with the dogs of my flock.
2. Even the strength of their hands, what is it to me?
    Their manly vigour is wasted away.

---

trees, which would otherwise never be able to resist the heat; but with this refreshment they thrive well and blossom, and ripen their fruit. Travels, p. 455.

20.—This figure is very common in Arabic poetry. See Schultens *in loco.*

22.—*Dropped upon them.*—As dew.

23.—*Harvest-rain.*—See Prov. xvi., v. 15, note. The idea is that the assembly desired him to speak, as a farmer desires the rain that will forward his crop.

24.—The idea is that his authority and character were so much reverenced, that his very smiles were received with awe.

25.—*Chose out heir way.*—I was their guide.

1.—*Younger than I.*—From chapter xv., v. 10, it would appear that Job does *not* refer here to his three friends.—*To rank.*—They were held in less esteem than his dogs. The Orientals had no language that would express greater contempt of any one than to call him a dog. See 1 Sam. xvii., v. 43; xxiv., v. 14; 2 Sam. iii., v. 8; ix., v. 8., and several other places.

2.—Translators and commentators differ greatly on this most difficult passage. Perhaps the idea is, that he could not employ such men, whose conduct was profligate, and who had become feeble through their vices.

3. Through want and severe famine,
   They were lately gnawing the desert,
   The waste and the wilderness;
4. Plucking up MALLUAH from the bushes,
   And RETEM-roots for their food;
5. They were driven from society;
   (Men shouted after them as after a thief;)
6. To dwell in the ravines of the torrents;
   In caves of the earth, and in the rocks;
7. Among the bushes they brayed;
   Under thorns they satisfied their sensuality;
8. As a profligate—as a base-born race,
   They were driven out of the land:
9. And now am *I* become their song;
   Yea, *I* am their by-word!
10. They abhor me, they stand aloof from me;
    They refrain not to spit before my face!
11. Because He hath loosed my nerve and afflicted me,
    They throw off the bridle in my presence!
12. On my right hand rise up a brood;
    They push away my feet;
    They cast up their destructive ways against me;
13. They break up my path,
    They further my ruin,
    Without benefit for themselves;

3.—Job says that he was treated with contempt by those who were reduced to the most abject wretchedness.

4.—*Malluah—Retem.*—Neither of these words I have translated. See Biblical Researches 1299; Burckhardt. Travels in Syria, p. 480; Smith's Biblical Dictionary on the words "Mallows" and "Juniper."

6.—*In the ravines.*—This exactly describes both the country of Stony Arabia, and the manners of its inhabitants. The rocks abound with caverns, and are to this day the abode of Arabian hordes.

7.—I have followed Professor Wolfsohn. This is an illustration of a state of society existing then.

8.—*Base-born race.*—Persons of obscure parentage, owned by no family, a spurious brood.

9.—*Their song.*—They made him the subject of low jesting.

11.—*Loosed my nerve.*—Destroyed my family and my property.—*They throw off.*—A common metaphor among the Arabs to denote: "To act without restraint."

14. As through a wide breach they advance;
    With tumult they roll themselves forward.
15. My eminence is changed into weakness;
    My dignity is chased away as the wind,
    And my safety is departed as a cloud;
16. Yea, now my soul melteth within me;
    For days of affliction have laid hold on me;
17. At night my bones are pierced through;
    My gnawing pains suffer me not to rest;——
18. With great force must my garment be stripped off;
    One could gird me with the collar of my tunic.
19. HE hath cast me into the mire;
    And I am become like dust and ashes.— — —
20. I cry unto Thee, but me Thou dost not answer;
    I stand up, but Thou dost not regard me;
21. Thou art become cruel unto me;
    With Thy strong hand Thou persecutest me;
22. Thou liftest me up,
    And causest me to ride on the wind;.
    And Thou then dissolvest my very substance.——
23. Indeed I know that Thou wilt bring me to death,
    To the house appointed for all living— — —
24. Yet on the ruins He will not lay his hand,
    If in its destruction there were an alleviation!——

14.—The translators of the A. V. supposed that the image was here taken from an inundation: more likely it is to an irruption made by a foe through a breach in a wall, the besieging army tumbling into the heart of the city.

16.—Pococke informs us, that the Arabians call a fearful person, one who has a watery heart, or whose heart melts away like water.

18.—*Be stripped off.*—Being glued, as it were, to the body by sores. This is the most natural interpretation of this most difficult passage, and there is no need for adding *three* words as in the A. V., which are not in the original.—*One could gird me.*—He was reduced to a skeleton; even the collar of his tunic would fit him round his body.

22.—See Taylor's Fragments in Calmet's Dictionary, vol. iii., p. 235. Rosenmüller supposes that the image is borrowed from a cloud floating through the atmosphere with the wind, till at last it dissolves into rain, and is seen no more. Coverdale renders: "In times past "thou didst set me up on high, as it were above the wind, but now hast "thou given me a very sore fall." Professor Wolfsohn nearly the same.

24.—This verse is very obscure; all commentators—Jewish and Christian—differ. According to my humble opinion Job says; "I

25. Did I not weep for him that was in trouble?
    Was not my soul grieved for the destitute?
26. When I looked for good, then evil came;
    When I expected light, then came darkness.
27. My bowels boil, and rest not;
    For days of affliction have anticipated me.
28. I am become black, but not by the sun;
    I stand up, and weep in the congregation.
29. A brother am I to the jackal;
    A companion to female ostriches;
30. My skin is black upon me,
    And my bones burn with heat;
31. My harp is turned to mourning,
    And my pipe to notes of grief.

---

know I shall die, but God will as yet not do me the favour to put an end to my misery, because *death* would be a relief to me." This is the "cruelty" of which he speaks in verse 21.

25.—Job says: "Did I deserve such a hard lot? Did I not show compassion to others? Why does God then not show compassion to me?"

26.—Job says: "I expected happiness, as the result of my benevolence; yet, instead of that, calamity came and swept all my comforts away."

27.—*My bowels boil.*—A metaphorical expression denoting extreme agitation and distress of mind.—*Anticipated.*—See ch. iii., v. 12.

28.—*Black.*—So Rashi and the Targum.—*Not by the sun.*—Reiske, Good, and Wolfsohn give the Arabic sense to the word "chamma," without *protection.*" This rendering suits the second part of this verse.

29.—*A brother am I.*—The text is equivalent to: "I am an outcast from human society, and associate or companion with such creatures only as live in solitude and deserts."—*Jackal.*—So Gesenius, Umbreit, and Noyes; an animal that abounds in deserts, and that makes a doleful cry in the night. Dr. Shaw was an ear-witness to the hideous noises which ostriches make in the night. "During the lonesome part of the night," says that entertaining traveller, "they often made very doleful and hideous noises, which would sometimes be like the roaring of a lion; at other times it would bear a nearer resemblance to the hoarser voice of other quadrupeds, particularly to that of the bull and the ox. I have often heard them groan as if they were in the greatest agonies." Travels, p. 450-455, 4to.

31.—*Pipe.*—*Ugab*, which the Chaldee renders *abuba.* Now *abub* in its primary sense signifies *an ear of corn;* and in its derivatives *abuba, anbuba,* and *ambubaja,* it comes to denote progressively in the lapse of ages, a *corn-pipe, a reed, a sonorous tube* of wood, brass, or other metal.

XXXI.
1. I made a covenant with mine eyes,
That I would not look on a maid.
2. For what portion could I have from God above,
What inheritance from the Almighty on high?
3. Is not destruction for the wicked,
And utter ruin to the workers of iniquity?
4. Doth not He see my ways,
And number all my steps?
5. If I have walked in falsehood,
And my foot hath hasted to deceit:—
(6. Let Him weigh me in the scales of justice,
And let God know mine integrity!)
7. If my step hath turned toward this course,
And mine heart hath followed mine eyes,
Or any stain hath cleaved to mine hands:
8. Then let me sow, and another eat;
Let what I plant be rooted up!
9. If my heart hath been enticed by a woman,
Or if I have lain wait at my neighbour's door:

1.—*I made a covenant.*—Job says, that he had resolved, in the most solemn manner, that he would not allow his eyes or thoughts to endanger him by improperly contemplating a woman. Heath is of opinion that the passage has a reference to a particular species of idolatry. The word "Betulah," which we render *maid*, he considers as the name of an idol. Eusebius informs us, from Sanchoniathon, that Ouranos was the first introducer of "Baitulia," when he erected *animated stones*, or, according to Bochart, *anointed stones*. The custom of anointing pillars, we know, was very ancient, for Jacob set up a pillar and anointed it. Gen. xxviii. Such stones were afterwards converted to idolatrous uses; and it was one of the commands to the children of Israel to break them to pieces, on their entrance in the land of Canaan. See Exod. xxxiv., v. 13.

2.—Job says, what reward could I expect from God, had I indulged impure desires. The question he answers himself in the next verse.

3.—*Utter ruin.*—Several Hebrew MSS. read "neched." This various reading is adopted by Schultens, which, in Arabic, signifies "every kind of misery."

5.—*In falsehood.*—The Sept.: "If I have walked with *scoffers*." This reading is confirmed by several Hebrew MSS.

8.—*Let what I plant.*—I have followed Schultens, Rosenmüller, Herder, Umbreit, and Lee. There is no evidence that he alludes here to his children.

9.—*Woman.*—A married woman.—*Lain wait.*—To watch when he would be absent from home.

10. Then may my wife grind for another,
    And may others cohabit with her;
11. For this would be a heinous crime;
    An iniquity punishable by the judges;
12. For it is a fire that would burn to destruction,
    And root out all my increase!
13. Have I refused justice to my man servant,
    Or my maid, when they had a suit with me?
(14. For what should I do, did God rise up;
    What could I answer, did He punish me?
15. Did not He that made me in the womb make him?
    Did He not fashion us in one womb?)
16. Have I denied to the poor their wish,
    Or caused the eyes of the widow to fail?
17. Or have I eaten my morsel alone,
    And the orphan hath not eaten of it?
(18. He, who was brought up with me,
    As though we were of one father;
    She, whose guide I was,
    As though she came out of my mother's womb?)

10.—The classical scholar who recollects the "ALIENAS PERMOLERE UXORES" of Horace (Lib. i., sat. ii., 35) and is acquainted with the construction of the ancient hand-mill, will have no doubt as to the meaning of this metaphorical expression. In this sense the Rabbinic writers understand this passage, as also Judg. xvi., v. 21; Sam. v., v. 13. The Targum and the Sept. understand this passage also in this sense.

12.—*For it is a fire.*—Which would bring upon me the heaviest calamities both from God and men.—Rosenmüller.

13-14.—Job says that he never refused to do justice to his servants, when they complained that his dealings with them had been severe; for he knew well that if he did injustice to them God would punish him, and he could have no excuse.—*Rise up.*—To judgment. The phraseology is taken from human judicatures. A judge usually stood up when he passed sentence.

15.—*Did not He.*—The equality of all men by nature is a strong argument against the abuse of those distinctions, which Divine Providence has established in the world for the good of society.

16.—*To fail.*—I have not frustrated the hopes of the widow, or disappointed her expectations, when she desired my aid.

18.—*He* refers to the orphan, *she* to the widow (v. 16). There is some difficulty in this verse, but I hope my rendering will satisfy the indulgent reader.

19. When I saw one wandering without clothing,
    Or a poor man without covering,
20. Did his loins not bless me,
    When warmed with the fleece of my sheep?
21. If I have lifted up my hand against the orphan,
    Because I saw my power in the gate:
22. Then may my shoulder fall from the blade,
    And mine arm be broken at the socket!
23. For destruction from God was a terror to me,
    And before His Majesty I could do nothing.
24. If I have made gold my trust,
    Or said to fine gold: "Thou art my confidence;"
25. If I rejoiced because my wealth was great,
    Or because my hand had found abundance;— —
26. If I beheld the sun when it shined,
    Or the moon advancing in her brightness,
27. And my heart hath been secretly enticed,
    And my mouth hath kissed my hand—:

19.— *Wandering.*—This is the true meaning of "obed." The word is applied to the sheep which has wandered from the fold, Psalm cxix., v. 176. The same rendering ought to be given to Deut. xxvi., v. 5, viz.: "A wandering Syrian." The common version is not appropriate to the condition of the patriarchs. They were not *ready to perish*, but were rich and prosperous. Abraham was a Syrian by birth, and, by the call of God, a wanderer from his kindred and country. Isaac and Jacob lived a like wandering life.

20. —*Loins.*—Equivalent to "his heart."

22.—There is a striking grandeur in this imprecation on the arm that was lifted up to threaten an orphan in a court of justice.

23.—*For destruction.*—The destruction which God would bring upon me awed and restrained me.

24.—*If I have made gold.*—If I have put my trust in *gold* rather than in *God*.

26.—*Beheld the sun.*—As an object of worship. Sabaism, or the worship of the heavenly bodies was the most ancient species of idolatry. The Arabs went early into it. They adored the sun, moon, planets, and fixed stars.

27.—*Kissed.*—Kissing the idol was an act of religious homage. See 1 Kings xix., v. 18. The heavenly bodies being at too remote a distance for a salute of the mouth, their worshippers substituted kissing their own hand in the place of that ceremony. See Niebuhr's Reisebeschreibung I., seite 414.

28. Even this were an iniquity punishable by the judge;
    For I should have denied the God who is above;
29. Did I rejoice at the destruction of mine enemy,
    Or exult when calamity befell him?
30. No! I suffered not my mouth to sin
    By imprecating a curse on his soul.
31. How often did not the men of my tent say:
    " O that we had of his meat!
    " We cannot be satisfied!"
32. No! the stranger did not lodge in the street;
    My door I opened to the traveller.——
33. Have I, as other men, covered my transgression,
    By concealing mine iniquity in my bosom?
34. Then I would dread the great multitude;
    The contempt of families would terrify me;
    I would be silent, and never go out of the door!——
35. O that I had one who would hear me!

26-28.—In Africa, on the first appearance of the new moon, which the Negroes look upon to be newly created, the Pagan natives, as well as the Mahometans, say a short prayer, and this seems to be the only visible adoration which the Kafirs (unbelievers) offer up to the Supreme Being. This prayer is pronounced in a whisper, the party holding up his hand before his face. Its purport is to return thanks to God for His kindness through the existence of the past moon, and to solicit a continuation of His favour during that of the new one. At the conclusion, they spit on their hands, and rub them over their faces. Mungo Park's Travels, p. 271. Among the Hebrews idolatry was an offence punishable by death, by stoning; Deut. xvii., v. 2-7. It is possible that in the time of Job it was regarded a heinous crime, and one of which the magistrate ought to take cognizance.—*Have denied.*—Polytheism is a direct denial of the unity of God.

31-32.—Nearly all translators differ, and interpreters are by no means agreed as to its meaning. Perhaps my explanation will satisfy the reader. Job refers to his hospitality, and says: "The men of my tent—*i.e.*, my servants—often said, when they saw that my house was always open to the travellers—'What shall *we* eat? We shall not be satisfied, because of these strangers who dine with him?'" But *I* did not listen to them, *I* did my duty, I entertained the traveller and lodged the stranger. This virtue was, and still is, the national character of the Arabs.

33.—*As other men.*—The Hebrew has no necessary reference to *Adam*, our first progenitor, who did *not* attempt to conceal or to cover his transgression.

Behold, my vindication! May the Almighty answer me!
Or let mine adversary write down the charge!
36. Surely, I would carry it on my shoulder,
And bind it around me as a diadem;
37. The number of my steps I would declare to him;
Like a prince would I approach him!——

38. If my land cry out against me,
And its furrows likewise complain;
39. If its produce I have eaten without payment,
Or grieved the soul of its managers:—
40. Then may it produce thistles instead of wheat,
And noxious weeds instead of barley!

(The pleadings of Job are ended).

PART 5.

CHAPTER XXXII.

1. So these three men ceased to answer Job, because he
2. was righteous in his own eyes. Then was kindled the wrath of Elihu, the son of Barachel the Buzite,

---

35.—*Adversary.*—My accuser; for an adversary in law is the plaintiff.

36.—*Carry it.*—The accusation. I know well, he says, that no charges can be brought against me which I could not exhibit publicly.

37.—*Declare to him.*—I would disclose to him the whole course of my life.—*Like a prince.*—I would not go bowed down under the consciousness of guilt, but with the firm and upright step with which a prince commonly walks.

38-40.—These verses are transferred from their proper place by an error of transcribers, and they should have been inserted after verse 23 or 34. The verses 35-37 make an appropriate and impressive close of the chapter.

1.—*Because he was righteous.*—This assigns the reason of the silence of Job's three friends. They looked upon him as too self-conceited and obstinate for conviction.

2.—*The Buzite.*—Buz was the second son of Nahor, the brother of Abraham (Gen. xxii., v. 20, 21.) Buz occurs but once as the name of a place or country (Jer. xxv., v. 23), where it is mentioned with Dedan

of the family of Ram; against Job was his wrath kindled, because he justified himself more than God;
3. also against his three friends was his wrath kindled, because they had found no answer, and yet they had
4. condemned Job. Now Elihu had waited for their reply to Job, because they were older than him-
5. self; but when Elihu saw that there was no answer in the mouth of these three men, then was his
6. wrath kindled; and Elihu, the son of Barachel the Buzite spoke, and said:
I am young, and ye are very old;
Therefore I trembled, and was afraid
To tell you mine opinion;
7. I thought: "Days should speak,
" And multitude of years teach wisdom."
8. But it is the spirit in man;
The inspiration of the Almighty giveth him understanding.
9. Great men are not always wise;
Neither do the aged always understand what is right;

---

and Tema. Dedan is a city of Idumea. Tema belonged to the children of Ishmael, who are said to have inhabited from Havilah unto Shur, which is in the district of Egypt; Gen. xxv., v. 15, 18. Tema is also mentioned in connection with Sheba; Job vi., v. 19. —*Of the family of Ram.*—According to Rashi and the Targum "Ram" is Abraham.—*More than God.*—He had defended his own innocence in such a manner as to represent God to have done him wrong.

3.—*And yet they had condemned Job.*—They held him to be guilty, and yet they were unable to adduce the proof of it, and to reply to what he had said. According to the Talmud this passage has been altered, it should have been, "and they *accused God*," viz., by their silence they confessed that Job was guiltless, and that God had done injustice to him. Aben Ezra, however, remarks: "Those who say that this passage has been altered know that which I do not."

6.—*I am young.*—For a *youth* to speak in such an assembly, on so delicate and difficult a subject, was an astonishing phenomenon in Arabia.

7.—*Days should speak.*—The aged ought to speak. They have had the advantage of long observation of the course of events.

8.—*It is the spirit.*—Not the *age* is it which gives wisdom to man; it is God's spirit which makes wise.

9.—*Great men.*—Men distinguished for rank and authority.

10. Therefore I say: "Hearken to me;
    "I also will declare mine opinion:"—
11. Behold, I waited for your words;
    I listened for your arguments,
    While ye searched out what to say;
12. Yea, your attestations I have considered,
    But lo! no one convinced Job;
    No one among you answered his words.
13. Do not say: "We have found wisdom;
    God only can subdue him—not man;"
14. No, had he directed his words against me,
    I would not with your speeches have answered him.
15. How they were amazed! they answered no more!
    Words were removed from them!—
16. I have waited but they speak not;
    Though they stand up, they make no reply:—
17. Now will *I* answer on my part;
    I also will show mine opinion;
18. For I am full of words;
    The spirit within constraineth me.
19. Behold, my bosom is as wine that hath no vent;
    As bottles of new wine it is ready to burst.

13.—*Do not say.*—The particle "pen" is interdictory or dissuasive.—*We have found wisdom.*—We were able to reply, but no *man* can convince him, *God* only can do so; therefore we remained silent.

15-16.—Here Elihu turns to the audience, desiring them to observe the confusion of the three seniors; who, though he had waited, had nothing to offer. That there were others present at the meeting of the three friends at Job's house is certain, for Elihu was present. This supposition, however, is not *absolutely* necessary, for it is not uncommon in Hebrew poetry to change from the second person to the third, especially where there is any censure or rebuke implied. See ch. xviii., v. 4.

18.—*I am full of words.*—He was so impressed with the subject, that it would be a relief for him to give utterance to his views.

19.—Elihu compares himself to a bottle in which new wine had been put, and where there was no vent for it, and when, in consequence, it was ready to burst. Bottles in the East are usually made of the skins of goats. The process of manufacturing them at present is this: the skins of the goats are stripped off whole, except at the neck. The holes at the feet and tail are sewed up. They are

20. I will speak that I may breathe more freely;
 I will open my lips and reply;
21. Now I will not accept any one's person,
 Nor give flattering titles to man;
22. For I know not—should I give flattering titles—
 How soon my Maker would take me away!

XXXIII.
1. Therefore, O Job, I pray thee, hear my discourse,
 And to all my words listen attentively!
2. Behold, now I open my mouth;
 My tongue now speaks in my mouth;
3. My words shall be in the uprightness of my heart,
 And my lips shall utter knowledge clearly;
4. The spirit of God hath made me;
 The breath of the Almighty hath given me life:
5. If thou art able, reply to me;
 Set thyself in order before me, stand up!
6. Behold, I, like thee, am a creature of God;
 I also am formed out of clay;
7. Therefore my terror dare not dismay thee,
 And my weight can not be burdensome to thee.——

first stuffed out full, and strained by driving in small billets and chips of oak wood, and then are filled with a strong infusion of oak bark for a short time, until the hair becomes fixed, and the skin sufficiently tanned.

2.—*In my mouth.*—Literally: " in my palate." This word may be used here, because of the importance of that organ in the act of speaking.

3.—*My words shall be.*—What I speak shall be the real suggestion of my heart; what I feel and know to be true. — *Utter knowledge clearly.* —I shall state things just as they are. His object is to guard himself from the suspicion of partiality.

4.—*The spirit of God.*—Elihu says that he is, like Job, a man; that both were formed in the same way, from the same breathing of the Almighty, and from the same clay; or that he had no occasion to fear that he would be overawed and confounded, for he could now conduct his cause *with a man* like himself. See ch. ix., v. 34, 35, and notes.

6.—Translators greatly differ. The rendering of the A. V. agrees with Rashi, but the parallelism requires a different rendering. I therefore follow Professor Wolfsohn, Noyes, and Umbreit.

7.—We cannot enter into the beauty of this delicate reprehension, unless we recollect those daring expressions in ch. ix., v. 34, 35; ch.

8. Surely thou hast said in my hearing,
   Yea, I have heard the sound of the words:
9. "I am pure, and without transgression;
   "I am clean, nor is there wickedness in me;
10. "Behold, He inventeth accusations against me;
    "He regardeth me as His enemy;
11. "He putteth my feet in the clog;
    "He watcheth all my paths."
12. Behold, in this thou art not right, I tell thee;
    For, as God is greater than man,
13. Why then dost thou strive against Him,
    Because He doth not give account of any of His doings?
14. Yet, God speaketh once, yea, twice,
    But man regardeth it not:——
15. In a dream, in a vision of the night,
    When deep sleep falleth upon men,
    In slumbering upon the bed——
16. Then He revealeth to the ears of men,
    The punishment which He hath sealed up for them;

xiii., v. 20-22.—*My weight.*—My dignity. Elihu says that he could speak to him as a friend, unawed and unterrified by any dread of overwhelming majesty and power.

9.—This is not the exact language which Job had used, and there seems to be some injustice done him in saying that he had employed such language. He had *not* intented to maintain that he was *absolutely free from sin.* See ch. ix., v. 20.

10.—*He regardeth me.*—This is the language which Job had used. See ch. xix., v. 11.

11.—*He putteth.*—See ch. xiii., v. 27.

12-13.—*For.*—The object is not to show *that* God was greater than man (as would seem from the Auth. Vers.), for that could not be a matter of information; but *because* He was far above man, he had no right to extort from Him a statement of the causes *why* He afflicts us. We are required to submit to *His will*, not *to our own reason.*

14.—*Once, yea, twice.*—Again and again.

15.—*In a dream.*—Compare Gen. xv., v. 12; xx., v. 6. Elihu instances in what manner God speaketh to and admonisheth men; first by dreams, and secondly by afflictions. At the same time, it is scarcely necessary to remark, that what is here and elsewhere said in the Scriptures about *dreams*, is no warrant for putting any confidence in them *now*, as if they were revelations from heaven.

16.—The idea is that God announces to them certain punishment if they continue in sin. So Rosenmüller and Wolfsohn.

17. That He may turn man from his evil work,
   And hide pride from the mighty;
18. To keep him back from the pit,
   And his life from perishing by the sword.——
19. Again he is warned by pain upon his bed;
   By the violent suffering of his bones;
20. So that his life abhorreth bread,
   And his soul the choicest food;
21. His flesh is consumed that it cannot be seen,
   And his bones which were invisible stick out;
22. And his soul draweth near to the pit,
   And his life to the destroying powers;
23. If then there be with him an angel,
   An intercessor—one among a thousand—
   To point out to the man his duty :

17.—God's *object* is to deter him from committing the deed of guilt which he had contemplated, and to turn him to the path of righteousness.

18.—*To keep him back.*—The *object* of these warnings is to keep him from rushing on to his own destruction.

19.—When the warnings of the night fail, and when he is still bent on a life of sin, then God lays him on a bed of pain, and he is brought to reflection there. There he has an opportunity to think of his life, and of all the consequences which would follow from a career of iniquity.

20, 21.—This is one of the common effects of disease. The design is to humble us, to take away the pride which delighted in the round and polished limb, the rose on the cheek, the ruby lip, and the smooth forehead, and to show us what we shall soon be in the grave.

23.—This part of Elihu's speech has given rise to scarcely less diversity of opinion, and scarcely less discussion than the passage in chapter xix., v. 25-27. Almost every interpreter has a peculiar view of its meaning, and of course it is very difficult to determine its true sense. The Vulg. renders it : " If there is for him an angel speaking —one of thousands—that he may announce the righteousness of the man, he will pity him and say : Deliver him that he descends not into corruption." Jerome (followed by Doederlein) seems thus to understand the passage as having a reference to the Jewish theology, which admits the doctrine of two classes of angels, the one *accusers*, the other *intercessors* for human frailty. His rendering, too, is admissible, for the original *may* be rendered : "to announce the righteousness of man," as well as "to point out to the man his duty" or righteousness. The Targum renders : " If there is merit in him, an angel is prepared, a *comforter*—paraclete (Greek, paracletos), that he may announce to man his rectitude, and he spares him, and says : Redeem him, &c." According to this paraphrast, God employs *angelic* beings

24. Then will He be gracious unto him, and say:
"Deliver him from going down to the pit;
"I have found a ransom:"
25. His flesh shall become fresher than a child's;
He shall return to the days of his youth;
26. Then prayeth he to God, who was merciful to him,
And appeareth joyfully before Him,
Who dealeth with mortal man in equity;
27. He singeth among men, and saith:
"I have sinned, and perverted that which was right;
"Yet He hath not dealt with me equal to my desert;

---

to communicate His will to men, and to assure them that He is willing to show mercy to them if they will repent. Maimonides (followed by Grotius) is of opinion that the passage refers to angels, regarded as mediators, who perform their office of mediation in two ways—by *admonishing* men, and by *praying* for them. Rashi seems to favour the opinion held by Jerome. The LXX. differ *too* much from the original, and of their opinion no idea can be formed. Professor Lee interprets the passage as referring to the founder of the Christian faith!! Le Clerc regards the passage as a mere *hypothesis* of Elihu, saying that *on the supposition* that an angel would thus visit men, they might be reclaimed. I have several other opinions before me, sufficient to form a separate volume, but most of them are unworthy of noticing. I also shall give *my* comment on this so much disputed passage:—Our sages say: "Man is always accompanied by *two angels; one* advising him to do good, *the other* advising him to do evil." (The reader will perceive that this is only a personification, and that the idea is that man has an *inclination* to do *good* and *evil*). With this saying of our sages, I shall endeavour to come to the true interpretation of this most difficult passage. Of that man who (according to verse 22) is lying on his mortal couch, Elihu says: "*If then there be for him an angel, an intercessor.*" That "angel" or "intercessor" is the *thought*, or the *inclination to repent.—One among a thousand.*—He having followed a career of iniquity, such a thought or inclination *to repent* is really "one among a thousand" *evil* inclinations which he had before he was laid prostrate on his bed.—*To point out to the man his duty.*—This duty is *repentance and prayer to God for pardon.* The idea of the whole verse is thus: "If that man is brought to reflection on his mortal couch, *repenteth*, and prayeth for pardon, then (v. 24) God will be gracious unto him, and say to the destroying powers (v. 22): 'Deliver him from going down to the pit, I have found a ransom or atonement; he has *repented;* this atones for his many sins which he had committed, and he shall return to his former health and strength."

25.—*Fresher than a child's.*—He will be restored again to health.—*To the days of his youth.*—To health and vigour.

27.—*He singeth.*—From "shir," to sing. So Schultens, Wolfsohn, and Umbreit. The connection requires this sense, though it *may*

28. "He hath delivered my soul from going down to the pit,
"And my life, that I might behold the light!"
29. Lo, all these things doth God
Twice, yea, thrice, with man,
30. To bring him back from the pit,
To enjoy the light of life.
31. Mark well, O Job, hear me;
Be silent, and I will speak;
32. But if thou hast anything to say, answer me;
Speak, for I desire to do thee justice;
33. If not, do thou listen to me;
Be silent, and I will teach thee wisdom.

CHAPTER XXXIV.

1. And Elihu proceeded, and said :
2. Hear my words, ye wise;
O ye that have knowledge, give ear unto me!
3. For the ear trieth words,
As the palate tasteth food;
4. That which is right let us choose to ourselves;
Let us know among ourselves what is best;

---

signify "to look," or "to observe."—*Equal to my desert.*—My afflictions were in no sense equal to my deserts. I have not been punished as I might justly have been.

28.—*My soul—my life.*—I have translated according to the "Kethiv."

33.—*Teach thee wisdom.*—He would still offer what Job himself would deem good sense and salutary instruction. It may be supposed that Elihu paused here to give Job an opportunity to reply; but as he made no reply, he resumed his discourse in the following chapter.

2.—*Ye wise.*—The previous chapter had been addressed to Job himself. He now addresses himself to his three friends. He speaks to them as "wise men," because he regarded them as qualified to understand the difficult subject which he proposed to explain.

3.—Elihu retorts what Job had said against his friends. Ch. xii., v. 11.

4.—*Let us choose.*—Amid the conflicting opinions and the sentiments which have been advanced, let us find out what will bear investigation.

5. For Job hath said: "I am righteous,
   " But God hath neglected my cause;
6. " However just may be my cause,
   " I appear to be a liar;
   " Mine arrow is mortal without transgression!"
7. Where is the man like Job,
   Who drinketh up scorning like water?
8. Who joineth himself to the workers of iniquity,
   Who walketh with wicked men?
9. For he hath said: "A man prospereth not
   " By delighting himself in God!"
10. Wherefore, ye men of understanding, hearken to me:
    Far be it from God to do wickedness;
    And injustice far from the Almighty!
11. For He will render to man his work,
    And requite every man according to his way.
12. Surely, God will not do wickedly,
    Nor will the Almighty pervert justice!

5.—*I am righteous.*—Compare ch. xiii., v. 18, and xxiii., v. 10, 11.—*Neglected my cause.*—See ch. xxvii., v. 2 and note.

6.—*However just.*—Translators vary. Sept: "He (God) hath been false in my accusations." Jerome: "For in judging me there is falsehood." Professor Lee: "Should I lie respecting my case?" i.e., "Shall I confess myself guilty, when I am not?" Noyes: "Though I am innocent, I am made a liar."—*Mine arrow.*—Durrel abandons the common version as indefensible, for "chetz" signifies *an arrow*, not a *wound*—The image is no doubt taken from an animal that had been pierced with a deadly arrow. Good takes the words "anoosh chitzi" in the Arabic sense, and renders: "He has reserved my lot without a trespass." This is agreeable to the context.—*Without transgression.*—Without any sin that deserved such treatment.

7.—*Scorning.*—Contemning the decrees of Providence; and the comparison indicates the habit of indulging it with the utmost freedom. A similar image occurs, ch. xv., v. 16.

9.—*He hath said.*—Not in so many words, but Elihu collects this as a fair inference from his speeches. See ch. xix., v. 10; xxix., v. 18; xxx., v. 21, 26.

10.—Elihu proceeds now to reply to what he regarded as the erroneous sentiments of Job. Still he does not meet the *facts* of the case, and he pursues substantially the same course as the friends of Job had done. The *facts* to which Job had referred are scarcely adverted to, and the perplexing questions are still unsolved.

11.—*He will render.*—He will treat each man as he deserves.

13. Who hath given Him charge over the earth ?
    Or who hath made the whole world ?
14. If He set His heart against him,
    And recall his spirit and his breath :
15. All flesh would expire together ;
    And man would return to the dust.
16. If thou hast understanding hear this !
    Hearken to the voice of my words !
17. Can one that hateth justice govern ?
    And wilt thou condemn Him that was always just ?
18. Who saith to a king : "Thou art a profligate ?"
    Or to princes : "Ye are wicked ?"
19. Much less to Him who favours not princes,
    Nor regardeth the rich more than the poor :
    For they all are the work of His hands.——
20. In a moment they die !
    At midnight are the people confounded, and pass away !
    The mighty are removed as well as the powerless :

13.—Elihu's first argument, to prove that God cannot be unjust is taken from His *independence*. God, he says, is under subjection to no one, hence He cannot be tempted to do wrong to gratify the feelings of his superior.

14-15.—Elihu argues now from the divine benevolence. If God were not benevolent, this earth, instead of being full of the goodness of the Lord, would become a dreadful scene of desolation ; instead of preserving he would extinguish the sinful race of man. According to Rosenmüller, the idea is : " If God should examine with strictness the life of man, and mark his faults, no flesh would be allowed to live. All would be found to be guilty, and would be cut off." Grotius, Umbreit, Schnurrer, Eichhorn, and Wolfsohn suppose it to mean : " If God should regard only Himself, if He wished to consult His own welfare, he would take away life from all, and live and reign alone."

16.—Elihu does not doubt whether Job had understanding, but admits it, and calls on him to exercise it.

18.—He illustrates his argument by the common practice of men, who speak not of Kings or princes disrespectfully.

20.—This verse is extremely obscure. In order to explain it, we may observe : I. That it is a confirmation of God's impartiality in his punishments by example. II. That the judgment is capital and instantaneous. III. That, to increase the terror, it is inflicted at midnight. (Rashi observes "as in Egypt"). IV. That it causes a general consternation. V. That the mighty perish by it as well as the powerless.—*As the powerless.*—So Professor Wolfsohn.

21. For His eyes are upon the ways of man;
    He seeth all his steps;
22. There is no darkness nor death-shade,
    Where workers of iniquity may hide themselves;
23. He needeth not, therefore, lay more upon man,
    In order to convict him at His tribunal.
24. Without inquiry He breaketh down the mighty,
    And setteth up others in their stead;
25. Because He knoweth their works,
    He bringeth night upon them;
26. They are crushed on account of their wickedness;
    He smiteth them in the presence of beholders;
27. Because they turned away from Him,
    And had no regard to His ways;
28. And caused the cry of the poor to come before Him;
    The cry of the oppressed He did hear.——
29. When He giveth quiet, who can cause trouble?
    When He hideth his face, who can behold Him?
    And this in respect to a nation and a man alike;
30. That the profligate should no more reign,
    Nor be snares to the people.

22.—*May hide themselves.*—So as not to be detected by God.

23.—*Not lay more.*—Impute more guilt to him; referring to what Job had said (as quoted by Elihu) ch. xxxiii., v. 10. So Rashi and Wolfsohn. Good, after Grotius and Reiske, considers "'od," *more*, as a *noun*, denoting a fixed time: "Behold! not to man hath he entrusted the time of coming into judgment with God." Bishop Stock would read "'ol," *a yoke*, instead of "'od," *more*.

24.—Elihu says if sometimes the mighty are broken down suddenly, it is not because God perverts justice, and judgeth without investigating the case; no, we may be sure that God—from whose eye nothing is hidden—has searched out their hearts.

25.—*He bringeth night.*—Calamity.

26.—This verse is very obscure. I follow Professor Wolfsohn, who joins the last word of verse 25 to verse 26.—*In the presence of beholders.*—Openly. Their sins had been committed *in secret*, but they are punished *publicly*.

29.—*Hideth His face.*—See ch. xiii., v. 24 and note.—*And this.*—The same laws respecting the sources of peace and happiness apply to both; neither can secure permanent peace and prosperity without Him.

30.—All this is done to prevent wicked men from ruling over the people.

31. Surely it is proper to say to God:
  "I repent; I will no more offend;
32. "What I see not, teach Thou me;
  "If I have done iniquity, I will do so no more."
33. Or shall He recompense according to thy mind?
  Whether thou refuse, or choose, and not I?
  Speak, therefore, what thou knowest!
34. Men of understanding will speak as I do,
  Every wise man who heareth my views will say:
35. "Job hath spoken without knowledge,
  "And his words were without prudence."
36. My desire is that Job may be fully tried,
  For making replies like wicked men;
37. For he hath added rebellion to his sin;
  He hath clapped his hands among us,
  And multiplied his words against God.

CHAPTER XXXV.

1. And Elihu proceeded and said:
2. Thinkest thou this to be right,
  When thou saidst: "My righteousness is more than God's?"

31.—There is much diversity of opinion about the meaning of this and the following verses. The idea seems to be that Elihu holds it for granted that calamities are the consequences of sin; man ought, therefore, to repent when afflicted.

33.—*According to thy mind.* Shall He consult thee how He is to treat men?—*And not I.*—Elihu uses the words, which he supposes God to speak. We might supply: "And not I, *saith God.*" This verse is very obscure. Schultens gives no less than *seventeen* interpretations, which have been proposed.

36.—*Like wicked men.*—So several Hebrew MSS. read. This is more agreeable to the amiable spirit of Elihu than the text.

37.—*He hath added rebellion.*—Job's discontent with the measures of Providence towards him broke out in his very first speech, grew more loud and vehement in the course of the dispute, and arrived to its height in his presumptuous challenge of God, ch. xxxi., v. 35-37—*Clappeth his hands.*—He has shown contempt for the sentiments of his friends.—*Multiplied words*—Again and again he gave utterance to his reproachful feelings against God.

2.—*My righteousness is more.*—Job had nowhere said this, but Elihu regarded it as the substance of what he had said, or thought that what he had said amounted to the same thing. See ix., v. 30-35; x., v. 13-15.

3. For thou askest what advantage it will be to thee;
   "What profit shall I have from my being without sin?"
4. But I will answer thee,
   And thy companions with thee.
5. Look up to the heavens, and see;
   And behold the clouds, which are high above thee!
6. If thou sinnest, what doest thou against Him?
   If thy transgressions be multiplied,
   What doest thou to Him?
7. If thou be righteous, what givest thou Him?
   Or what receiveth He from thy hand?
8. Thy wickedness can injure only a man like thyself;
   Thy righteousness profit only a son of man.
9. The oppressed are made to cry on account of the multitude of wrongs;
   They cry out on account of the arm of the mighty;
10. Yet no one said: "Where is God, my Maker,
    " Who alloweth this tyranny every night?

3.—The rendering and punctuation of this verse is fully in accordance with the original, and it removes the difficulty which translators find in the words "to thee."——

4.—*And thy companions.*—Who remained silent, and did not reply.

5.—*Look up.*—The object of the reply is to show, that God is so great, that He cannot be affected with human conduct; that He is so exalted that man's conduct cannot affect His happiness. Look to the heavens, he says, so lofty, grand, and sublime, and *He* is above all those heavens, *He* cannot be affected by the righteousness or wickedness of man; wherefore dost thou then boast of thy righteousness?

6-7.—The object of Elihu is to show that God is not influenced in His treatment of His creatures, as men are in their treatment of each other. God has no *interest* in treating them otherwise than as they deserve.

8.—*Can injure.*—It may injure *man*, but not *God.* He is too independent of man in His sources of happiness, to be affected by what he can do. Neither man's good or evil conduct can affect Him.

9.—Elihu admits the facts to which Job had adverted (ch. xxiv.) that men *are* borne down by oppression, and that God does *not* interpose to save them. He admits that multitudes *do* thus suffer under the arm of oppression, and God does *not* interpose to rescue them. But he says: "Not even the vulgar venture to utter the blasphemy: 'There is neither judge nor justice!'" Much less shouldst *thou*, a magistrate, a man of knowledge—utter such words.—He should know, that though God does not punish the wicked *immediately*, they will meet the rewards of their wickedness hereafter.

11. "He wisheth us to be more intelligent than the beasts of the earth,
"And wiser than the fowls of the air:
12. "And yet people cry on account of the violence of the wicked,
"But He answereth not!
13. "Surely, it is conceit, God heareth not;
"The Almighty doth not regard it!"
14. Much less shouldst thou say thou seest Him not!
Justice is with Him; only wait thou for Him.
15. Or should He—because His anger resenteth not immediately—
Not take notice of the transgression?
16. How foolishly Job hath spoken!
Multiplying words without sense!

CHAPTER XXXVI.

1. Elihu also proceeded, and said:
2. Wait yet a little, and I will show thee,
That I have yet arguments on behalf of God;

14.—*Thou seest Him not.*—See ch. xxiii., v. 8. The fact that God is invisible should not be regarded as any evidence that He does not attend to the affairs of men.—*Wait thou for Him.*—Wait for the time when the now *invisible* God will interpose in thy behalf.——

The attentive reader will observe that from verse 9 until the end of the chapter I am at variance with nearly all translators. A careful examination, however, will convince that I have given a clear connection, without violating the original.

1.—*Proceeded.*—Hebrew: "added." The Hebrew commentators remark that the word "added" is used because this speech is *added* to the number which it might be supposed he would make. There had been *three* series of speeches by Job and his friends, and in each one of them Job had spoken *three* times. Each one of the three friends had also spoken *thrice*. Elihu had also now made *three* speeches; therefore it is remarked that he *added* this to the usual number.

2.—*Wait yet a little.*—Rashi remarks that this verse is Chaldaic. The word "Katar" has here a signification which occurs only in Syriac and Chaldee, viz.: *to wait.*—*That I have yet arguments.*—Elihu says that there were yet many considerations which could be urged in vindication of His government.

3. I will bring my knowledge from afar,
   To defend the righteousness of my Maker;
4. Yet my words shall not be false;
   One perfect in knowledge is with thee.
5. Behold, God is mighty, and despiseth no one;
   He is mighty in power and wisdom;
6. He preserveth not the life of the wicked;
   He doth justice to the oppressed;
7. He withdraweth not His eyes from the righteous,
   But with kings are they upon the throne;
   He establisheth them for ever, and they are exalted.
8. And if they are bound with fetters,
   And holden in the cords of affliction:
9. Then He showeth them their deeds,
   And how their transgressions have prevailed;

3.—*Bring my knowledge from afar.*—I will enter more deeply into the subject of the Divine justice.

4.—*Not be false.*—Job had charged his friends with making use of unsound arguments in vindicating His cause (ch. xiii., v. 7-8); Elihu now says that *he* will make use of no such reasoning, and that he would state nothing but what would bear the most rigid examination. —*One perfect in knowledge.*—One who will honestly speak the sentiments of truth in discoursing with thee. Elihu speaks of himself.—

5.—*Despiseth.*—"To despise," here means to take up an aversion against a person without cause, from caprice. He refers to Job's expressions, ch. x., v. 3.—

6.—*The life.*—Because he may happen to be rich and powerful. "Life" here means, or comprehends, everything that renders life desirable.

7.—*Withdraweth not.*—Elihu says, that the righteous are afflicted, but not forsaken.—*But with kings.*—They will receive the highest earthly honour.—Good thinks that the term "tzaddik" here signifies, "one who dispenses justice to another, a justifier, or judge." He renders: "He withdraweth not his eyes from the judge, nor from kings on the throne."

8.—*And if they.*—If the righteous are chained down, as it were, on a bed of pain, or crushed by heavy calamities.

9.—*He showeth them their deeds.*—Elihu says, that the object of their affliction is to bring them to see what their conduct has been, and to reform what has been amiss.—*Have prevailed.*—Therefore it was necessary to interpose in this manner, and check them by severe affliction.

10. He openeth also their ear to instruction,
   And commandeth them to turn from iniquity;
11. If they obey, and serve Him,
   They shall spend their days in prosperity,
   And their years in pleasures;
12. But if they obey not,
   They shall perish by the sword,
   And they shall die without knowledge.——
13. But the depraved in heart heap up wrath;
   They cry not when He bindeth them;
14. They die in their youth,
   And their life perisheth among the unclean.
15. He delivereth the afflicted from their affliction,
   When by suffering they are admonished.
16. Even so will He raise thee from distress;
   Wide, not strait, will be thy place,
   And the provision of thy table full of fatness;
17. But if thou art full of the sentiments of the wicked,

10.—*To instruction.*—To learn the lessons which their afflictions are designed to teach.

11.—Elihu says, the design of affliction is not to cut them off, but to bring them to repentance. The object was to assure Job, that he should not regard his calamities either as proof that he never understood religion—as his friends maintained, or that God was severe and did not regard those that loved and obeyed Him—as Job had seemed to suppose; but that there was something in his life which made discipline necessary, and that if he would repent of that, he would end his days in happiness and peace.

12.—*By the sword.*—By a signal judgment from God.

13.—*Heap up wrath.*—They remain impenitent, and are rebellious at heart, and they do not cry to God with the language of penitence when He binds them down by calamities.

14.—*Among the unclean.*—See Deut. xxiii., v. 17. Their criminal lusts and indulgences bring them to a premature end.

15.—*He delivereth.*—This assertion leads Elihu to address Job in strong but pertinent language.

16.—*Wide, not strait.*—Afflictions are compared with a narrow path, in which it is impossible to get along; prosperity with a broad and open road, in which there are no obstructions.

17.—I have followed Umbreit, who renders:

"Doch wenn du voll bist von des Frevlers Urtheil,
"So werden Urtheil und Gericht schnell auf einander folgen."

Then sentiments and justice will rapidly follow each other;
18. For there is wrath; beware
Lest He take thee away with a stroke;
Then a great ransom will not save thee.
19. Will He esteem thy riches?——
Neither wealth, nor all the exertions of power.
20. Pant not thou for the night,
In which nations are taken away to their place!
21. Take heed, lest thou return to iniquity;
For this thou hast preferred to affliction.——
22. Behold, God is axalted in His power;
Who is omniscient like Him?
23. Who hath appointed Him His way?
Or who can say: "Thou hast done wrong?"
24. Remember! thou shouldst magnify His work
Which men celebrate;

The idea is that if Job held the opinions of wicked men, he must expect that these opinions would be rapidly followed by judgment. This seems to express the thought which Elihu meant to convey.

18.—*There is wrath.*—Because God's wrath is justly excited on such occasions, beware.—*A great ransom*—Would not prevent him from being cut off.

19.—*Not wealth.*—Will save a man from the grave, if he be rebellious in affliction.

20.—*For the night.*—The night of death; the darkness of the grave. He most probably refers to ch. vii., v. 15, where Job had said: "Hence my soul chooseth strangling—Death—rather than my present life."—*In which nations.*—How many renderings have been given of this line! Schultens enumerates not less than fifteen different interpretations, and then remarks, that he "waits for clearer light to overcome the shades of *this* night." I have followed Noyes, but I confess I do not understand the passage as it stands in the original. Umbreit renders: "Pant not for the night, to go down to the people who dwell under thee." This would agree very well with the context, but the Hebrew will not bear this rendering.

21.—*Lest thou return.*—To the foolish and impious habit of arraigning the righteous judgments of God.—*Preferred.*—Rather than learn the humble duty of suffering affliction with patience and resignation.

23.—*Appointed.*—Who is superior to Him, and has marked out for Him the plan which He ought to pursue?

25. All men contemplate it;
Mortals behold it from afar.
26. Lo! God is great and we cannot comprehend Him;
The number of His years is unsearchable.
27. For He draweth up the drops of water;
They distil rain in its vapour
28. Which the clouds pour down;
They pour it upon man in abundance.
29. Yea, who understandeth the spreading of the clouds?
The fearful thunderings in His tent?
30. Lo! He spreadeth the lightning around Himself,
And concealeth it in the depths of the sea!

25.—*Contemplate it.*—The creation—*From afar.*—His works are so great and glorious that they make an impression even at a vast distance.

26.—*Comprehend Him.*—The creation demonstrates its author to be an eternal, almighty, incomprehensible being.—*Unsearchable.*—He is eternal.

27-28.—*He draweth up.*—Evaporation is the gradual solution of water in air, produced and promoted by attraction, heat, and motion, by which other solutions are effected. The attractive power of the air draws up the watery particles that are in contact with it. By attracting them, the air at the same time fineth them; separating and leaving behind their saline and other heterogeneous parts. By this Divine chemistry, they become qualified for the purposes of a rainy cloud. When the air has drawn up the watery vapours, it dissolves them; that is, unites them with itself. It keeps them suspended, in this state of solution, until by cold, or some other cause, it is forced to let some of them go. Then they ran together by their own mutual attraction, and form a cloud. They continue in that form until the cloud is so accumulated, by a fresh accession of more watery vapors, as to become heavier than the air; or until by heat or density the air itself is so diminished, as to become lighter than the cloud. The cloud then falls in drops of rain. Yet, who can define the precise bulk and shape of those minute particles of air, which are endowed with an attractive power? And, as for heat and cold, so instrumental in producing rain, who knows what are the first natural causes of them? Rain, therefore, which is the origin of fountains and rivers, and one principal means of carrying on vegetation, and supporting animal life, must still be reckoned among the great and incomprehensible works of God.

29.—*Who understandeth.*—In the early periods of the world, it could not be expected that the causes of these phenomena would be known. Now that the causes *are* better known, however, they do not less indicate the wisdom and power of God.

30.—*Around Himself.*—The lightning bursts from the cloud, the thick darkness in which He is supposed to dwell.

31. Verily, by them He judgeth the nations;
    By them He giveth food in abundance.——
32. The lightning covereth the whole sky,
    And He commandeth it where to strike;
33. By it He announceth His will,
    The fury of His wrath against the impious!

XXXVII.
1. My heart also trembleth at this,
   And is moved out of its place.
2. Hear, Oh hear the thunder of His voice,
   And the sound which goeth out of His mouth!

31.—*By them He judgeth.*—By means of the clouds, the rain, the tempest, and the thunderbolt. He can cause the tornado to sweep over the earth; He can withhold rain and dew, and spread over a land the miseries of a famine.—*He giveth food.*—By the clouds, the dew, and the rain, He can send timely showers, and the earth will be clothed with plenty.

32-33.—The translators of the authorized version did not understand this passage, and were not able to make out of it any tolerable sense. They render:

32.—"With clouds he covereth the light, and commandeth it *not* to shine, by *the cloud* that cometh betwixt."

33.—"The noise thereof showeth concerning it, the cattle also concerning the vapour." What idea they attached to the passage it would be very difficult to imagine. What can be the meaning of the phrase "the cattle also concerning the vapour?"—The object of Elihu is to excite admiration of the greatness of God, who is able thus to control the lightning's flash, and to make it an obedient instrument in His hands. Perhaps at the very moment that Elihu was speaking, Elihu saw a tempest rising; the first and second verses of the next chapter favour such an interpretation.—*To strike.* This is the sense of the verb "pagá." Compare Exod. v., v. 3; I Kings, ii., v. 25.

32.—*By it.*—The lightning is under God's direction, and He makes it the means of executing His will. See verse 30.

1.—*My heart also.*—Elihu sees a tempest rising. The clouds gather, the lightnings flash, the thunder rolls, and he is awed as with the conscious presence of God.—The former chapter very improperly terminates in the midst of this fine description of the thunder-storm.

2.—*Hear.*—It has been supposed by many, and not without probability, that the tempest was already seen rising, out of which God was to address Job (chap. xxxviii.) and that Elihu here calls the special attention of his hearers to the gathering storm, and to the low muttering thunder in the distance. Such an incident would greatly heighten the propriety and animation of this sublime description

3. Under the whole heavens is its flash,
And its lightning unto the ends of the earth;
4. After it, the thunder roareth;
He thundereth with the voice of His majesty,
And there is no limit to them when His voice soundeth.
5. God thundereth marvellously with His voice;
He doeth great things which we comprehend not!
6. For He saith to the snow: "Be thou on the earth;"
To the gentle rain: "Drop copiously;"
And to rain-storms: "Be ye violent!"
7. Thus He sealeth up the hand of every man,
That all men may know His work.
8. Then the wild beasts go to their dens,
And quietly rest in their caverns.
9. Out of the South cometh the whirlwind,

3.—*Ends.*—Hebrew: "wings." The word *wings* is given to earth, from the idea of its being spread out or expanded like the wings of a bird.

4.—*After it.*—After the lightning; that is, the flash is seen before the thunder is heard.—*No limit.*—So Good.

5.—*Great things.*—Not only in regard to the thunder and the tempest, but in other things.—The description of the storm ends here.—One of the most sublime descriptions of a storm to be found anywhere, is furnished by Klopstock. It is in the "Frühlingsfeier."

"Wolken strömen herauf!
Sichtbar ist; der kommt, der Ewige!

Nun schweben sie, rauschen sie, wirbeln die Winde!
Wie beugt sich der Wald! Wie hebet sich der Strom!
Sichtbar, wie du es der Sterblichen seyn kannst,
Ja, das bist du, sichtbar, Unendlicher!

Zürnest du, Herr,
Weil Nacht dein Gewand ist?
Diese Nacht ist segen der Erde.
Vater, du zürnest nicht!

Seht ihr den Zeugen des Nahen, den zükkenden Strahl?
Hört ihr Jehova's Donner? etc., etc."

7.—*He sealeth up.*—The lands being laid under water by these heavy and continual rains, a stop is thereby put to the works of the field.

8.—*The wild beasts.*—The low grounds being covered with water, the beasts of prey flee to the caverns of the mountains for safety.

9.—*Out of the South.*—M. Savary, speaking of the southern wind, which blows in Egypt from February to May, says: "It fills the

And cold from the Northern winds.
10. By the breath of God, the frost is produced,
 And the broad waters become congealed.
11. Again, His splendour dispelleth the thick cloud,
 And His light disperseth the extended cloud;
12. Thus revolveth He the seasons in His wisdom;
 That they may do whatever He commandeth them,
 Upon the habitable parts of the world;
13. Whether for correction, or for mercy,
 He causeth them to come on the earth.
14. Give ear to this, O Job! stand still,
 And consider the wondrous works of God!
15. Knowest thou how God disposeth them,
 When He causeth His luminous cloud to shine?
16. Knowest thou the balancings of the clouds,
 The wondrous works of perfect wisdom?
17. Or how thy garments become warm,

atmosphere with a subtil dust, which impedes respiration and brings with it pernicious vapours; sometimes it appears only in the shape of an impetuous whirlwind, which passes rapidly, and is fatal to the traveller, surprised in the middle of the deserts. Torrents of burning sand roll before it; the firmament is enveloped in a thick veil, and the sun appears red as blood. Sometimes whole caravans are buried in it." See Burder, in Rosenmüller's Alte u. neue Morgenland, No. 765.

10.—*By the breath of God.*—The stormy, cold, freezing winds, mentioned in the preceding verse. A tempestuous wind is, in the lofty style of eastern poetry, called "the breath of God."

11.—*His splendour.*—So the Targum, Schultens, and many of the best modern critics. Here we have a picture of the sky, in a clear, sharp, freezing day.

13.—I have transposed the order of the words, for no clear and consistent sense can be given of them as they now stand in the original. Good's fanciful etymology of "Shebet" and "crets," and the sense he attributes is unworthy his sagacity and general excellence.

15.—*Disposeth them.*—The winds, the clouds, the sky, the snow.—*His luminous cloud.*—Perhaps this refers to the rainbow.

16.—*The balancings.*—The clouds remain suspended, so long as their pressure is exactly balanced by the counter-pressure of the air, which is underneath them. But the law of the equilibrium, and the causes which destroy the balance, are so mysterious in their operation, that our knowledge of these matters is extremely superficial.

17.—*How thy garments.*—Some suppose that Elihu asks this question sarcastically; but there is every reason to believe that the

When He quieteth the earth by the South wind?
18. Hast thou with Him spread out the sky,
Which is strong as the molten mirror?
19. Teach us then what we shall say to Him;
We cannot address Him by reason of darkness.— —
20. Or must it be told to Him that I speak?
If a man speak, is it hidden from Him?
21. And now—men cannot behold the light,
When it is resplendent in the sky;
For the wind passeth along, and maketh it bright!
22. Golden splendour approacheth from the North;
How awful is the majesty of God!
23. The Almighty!—we cannot find Him out!
Great in power, and in justice!
Vast in righteousness! He doth not oppress!

question was proposed with entire seriousness, and that it was supposed to involve real difficulty.

18.—*With Him.*—Wert thou employed with God in performing that vast work, that thou canst explain how it was done?—*Molten mirror.*—The mirrors of the Israelitish women (Exod. xxxviii., v. 8,) were made of plates of metal, highly polished.

19.—*Teach us.*—The author here gives us an evident proof of his great skill in the management of the Drama, as he, by degrees prepares us for the appearance of the Almighty. His awful harbingers, the thunder and lightning, at a distance, had announced His coming. Elihu then trembled, and his heart was moved out of its place (v. 1,) but at His nearer approach, he is in the utmost hurry and confusion; he is afraid to open his mouth; he is lost in amazement; the glory of God is too dazzling for mortal eye to bear.

20.—*Must it be told.*—Does God not *know* all our thoughts? The idea of this verse is the same as Psalm cxxxix., v. 4.

21.—Elihu's language here becomes abrupt and confused. His language is just such as one would have used when the mind was overawed with the approach of God—solemn and full of reverence, but not connected, and much less calm than in his ordinary discourse. *Maketh it bright.*—The wind appeareth to pass along, removing the cloud which seemed to be a veil on the throne of God, and suffering His Majesty to be seen through the opening.

22.—*Golden splendour.*—Elihu now sees God approaching from the north; his mind is overawed; hence his discourse is so broken and disconnected.

23.—*Find Him out.*—His nature is incomprehensible, and the reasons of His dispensations equally so; yet everything proves that He is great in power, justice, and righteousness.—*He doth not oppress.* —He rebukes Job.

24. Wherefore men should reverence Him!
But many a wise man will not regard it.— — —

Part 6.

CHAPTER XXXVIII.

1. Then the Lord answered Job out of the whirlwind and said:
2. Who is this that darkeneth counsel
By speeches without knowledge?
3. Gird now manfully thy loins;
I will question thee, and answer thou Me.
4. Where wast thou when I founded the earth?
Declare :—doubtless thou knowest the plan!
5. Who then fixed its proportions? For thou knowest!
Or who stretched the line upon it?
6. Upon what are its foundations settled?
Or who laid its corner-stone,
7. When the morning stars sang together,
And all the sons of God shouted for joy?——

24.—*Many a wise.*—Here also he rebukes Job.

1.—While the lightnings were playing, and the thunders rolling, a bright, golden light is seen in the north, indicating the approach of the Most High. Elihu is overpowered with His majesty, and concludes his speech in a brief, hurried, and agitated manner. While he is thus speaking, God appears, and addresses Job from the midst of the storm, and puts an end to this protracted controversy.

2.—*Darkeneth counsel.*—By *counsel* is meant, that by which God governs the affairs of men. Job is said to darken it, because he mistook and misrepresented it.

4.—*Declare.*—Explain the manner in which the earth was formed and fixed in its place, and by which the world grew up under God's hand.—*Doubtless.*—I consider "im" as an affirmative particle.

5.—*For thou knowest.*—This expression is ironical, and is designed to rebuke Job's pretensions of being able to explain the Divine administration.—*Stretched the line.*—The earth is represented as a building, the plan of which was laid out beforehand, and which was then made according to the sketch of the architect. It is not, therefore, the work of chance or fate.

7.—*Morning stars.*—The Targum: "the stars of the Zephyr." This may be understood in its literal sense. Comp. Ps. cxlviii, v. 3.

8. Who shut up the sea with gates,
   In its bursting forth from the womb?
9. When I made the cloud its mantle,
   And thick darkness its swaddling-band?
10. When I measured boundaries for it,
    And fixed its bars and doors,
11. And said: "Thus far shalt thou come, but no farther,
    And here shall thy proud waves be stayed?——
12. Hast thou, since the day of thy birth,
    Commanded that it be morning?
    Or caused the dawn to know its place,
13. That it may seize on the ends of the earth,
    And shake the wicked out of it?

8.—*Shut up.*—Who restrained and fixed its bounds.—*The womb.* This must here mean the cavities of the earth, whence the water issued, when they were collected into their common receptacle.

9.—*Swaddling-band.*—The author had compared the eruption of the sea to the breaking forth of an infant from the womb. This image gave rise to the "mantle" and the "swaddling-band," to which he resembled those thick and dark clouds, which frequently arise over the sea and encompass it.

10.—*When I measured.*—Compare Prov. viii., v. 29: "When He appointed to the sea its bounds, that the waters should not pass its shore."—*Fixed its bars.*—God fixed the limit which they are not to pass.

12.—The transition from the *sea* to the *morning* is not so abrupt as it appears. For the ancients thought that the sun set in the ocean, and at his rising came out of it again.—*Since the days of thy birth.*—So Rashi, and so I have rendered "Yom" ch. iii., v. 1.—*That it be morning.*—So Aben Ezra.—*The dawn.*—The Aurora; the morning. At one season of the year it appears on the equator, at another north, and at another south of it; and is constantly varying its position, yet it always knows its *place.* It never fails to appear where, by the long-observed laws, it ought to appear.

13.—*Seize.*—The diffusion of the morning light over the whole face of the earth is expressed by the beautiful figure of its "seizing on the ends of the earth."—*And shake the wicked out of it.*—The moral benefit of the morning to mankind is taken notice of. "To shake the wicked out of it;" *i.e. to banish,* or *put to death.* In those times and countries, the court of justice sat in the morning.—See Judges vi., v. 31; Ps. ci., v. 8. This singular circumstance gives a dignity and importance to the description of the morning, worthy to come from the mouth of the righteous Governor of the world; or it may mean that the light of the morning drives them to their caves and lurking places.

14. That it may change [the earth] as clay by the seal,
    And all things stand as if in full attire?
15. That from the wicked their light be withheld,
    And the high arm be broken?
16. Hast thou penetrated the cliffs of the sea,
    Or walked through the depths of the abyss?
17. Have the gates of death been opened to thee——
    Yea, the gates of death-shade hast thou seen?
18. Hast thou considered the breadth of the earth?
    Declare:—doubtless thou knowest it all.
19. Where is the region which light inhabiteth?
    And the darkness—where is its place?
20. Surely thou canst take us to its boundary;
    Surely thou knowest the paths to its dwelling!
21. Thou knowest all this, because thou wast then born,
    And great is the number of thy days.——

14.—Schultens enumerates *twenty* interpretations of this passage, and of course it is not easy to determine the meaning. The idea probably is that during the darkness of the night, the earth is a perfect blank; in which state it resembles clay that has no impression. But the morning light falling upon the earth, innumerable objects make their appearance on it; it is then changed like clay which has received the stamp of the seal.—*Clay* was often used for the purpose of a seal in oriental countries.—See Harmer, vol. iv., page 385. The proper place of this verse is after verse 12.

15.—*May be deprived.*—*Night* is day for the wicked; hence when the light shines upon the world, the wicked, accustomed to perform their deeds in the night, flee from it, and retreat from their dark hiding places.—*High arm.*—The arm that is raised to commit some act of robbery or violence.

17.—*Gates of death.*—The gates that lead to the abodes of the dead.—It is common in the classic writers to represent those regions as entered by gates. Thus, Lucretius, I., 1105:

"——Haec rebus erit pars janua leti,
Hac se turba foras dabit omnis materaï."

"——The doors of death are open,
And the vast whole unbounded ruin whelms."—Good.

19.—Light and darkness are here personified; each has its separate dwelling. The bounds of one never encroach on those of the other.

20-21.—This is to be understood ironically. 21.—*Because thou wast then born.*—Thou must know all this, for thou art so old, and hast had an opportunity of observing all this.

22. Hast thou seen the storehouse of snow,
   Or seen the storehouse of hail,
23. Which I have reserved for the time of calamity,
   For the day of battle, and of war?——
24. By what way is the light divided?
   How is the east wind scattered on the earth?
25. Who hath laid out for the flood its channel,
   And who hath made a path for the thunder-flash;
26. To give rain to a land, where no man is;
   Upon a desert, where no man dwelleth;
27. To drench the dreary, desolate waste,
   And cause the bud of the tender herb to spring forth?

22.—*Storehouse of snow—hail.*—Snow and hail are here represented as if they were reserved in store-houses, like the weapons of war, to be called for when God should please, in order to execute His purposes. The appeal to Job here is, whether he could explain the phenomena of snow and hail? Could he tell how they were formed? Whence they came? Where they were preserved, and how they were sent forth to execute the purposes of God?—The effect of the discoveries which *are* made in the works of God is not to diminish our sense of His wisdom and majesty, but to change mere wonder to praise; to transform blind amazement to intelligent adoration.

23.—*Time of calamity.*—Leo Africanus assures us that the caravans which travel through the African deserts are sometimes suddenly overtaken with such furious storms of snow, that their beasts and carriages, and themselves, are burried in it.—*Battle—war.*—Hailstones were sometimes employed by God to overwhelm His foes, and were sent against them in time of battle. See Josh. x., v. 11.

24.—*Is the light divided.*—The light of the morning, that seems to come from one point, and to spread itself at once over the whole earth.—*How is the east wind.*—There is no reason to suppose that the spread of the light has any particular agency in causing the east wind, as the translators of the Auth. Vers. seem to suppose, nor is that idea necessarily in the Hebrew text. The idea is that the east wind, like the light, comes from a certain point, and seems to spread abroad over the world; and the question is, whether Job could explain this? Herder renders this verse:
"When doth the light divide itself,
   When the east wind streweth it upon the earth?"
According to his rendering the idea is that the light of the morning seemed to be borne along by the wind. —

25.—*Made a path.*—A path seems to be opened in the dark cloud for the passage of the flash of lightning.

26.—*Where no man is.*—This circumstance is dwelt upon to shew the provision which the Creator makes for the sustenance of wild beasts.

28. Who is the father of the rain ?
   Or who hath begotten the drops of dew ?
29. Out of whose womb cometh the ice ?
   The hoar-frost of heaven—who gave it birth ?
30. How do the waters become hard like a stone—
   The surface of the water—how is it congealed ?
31. Hast thou bound the bands of Pleiades,
   Or loosed the bands of Orion ?
32. Canst thou bring forth the celestial signs,
   Or canst thou guide Arcturus with his sons ?
33. Knowest thou the ordinances of heaven ?
   Appointedst thou their dominion over the earth ?
34. Canst thou lift up thy voice to the clouds,
   That an abundance of water may cover thee ?
35. Canst thou send forth lightnings ?
   Will they come and say to thee : " Here we are ? "
36. Who hath put wisdom into the shooting stars ?
   Or who hath given prudence to meteors ?

31.—*The bands of Pleiades.*—The question is, whether Job had created the *band* which unites the stars composing that constellation in so close union. So Wolfsohn, Rosenmüller, Umbreit, and Noyes. The word "bands" applied to the Pleiades is not unfrequently used in Persian poetry. Sadi, in his Gulistan, p. 22 (Amsterdam, 1651), speaking of a garden, says : " The earth is strewed, as it were, with emeralds, and the *bands of Pleiades* appear upon the boughs of the trees." So Hafiz, in one of his odes, says : " Over thy songs heaven has strewed the *bands of Pleiades* as a seal of immortality." See Rosenmüller's *Alte und neue Morgenland*, No. 768.

32.—*With his sons.*—The "sons" are the stars that accompany it, probably the stars that are now called the "tail of the bear." Umbreit.

33.—*The ordinances of heaven.*—By "heaven" is meant the celestial sphere, or the heavenly bodies contained in it. "The ordinances of heaven" are the laws by which those bodies perform their revolutions. These were wholly unknown in the time of Job.—*Their dominion.*—The influence of the heavenly bodies upon sublunary objects.

34.—Canst thou command the clouds so that they shall send down abundant rain ?

35.—*Here we are.*—This surprising figure of speech expresseth with great sublimity, the punctuality with which inanimate creatures observe the laws prescribed to them, and perform the service enjoined them by their Creator.

36.—There is great variety in the interpretation of this passage. Herder : " Who gave understanding to the flying clouds ? Or intelli-

37. Who can number the clouds by his wisdom
    And who can pour out the bottles of heaven.
38. So that the dust is turned into mire,
    And the clods cleave fast together?———

39. Canst thou hunt for the lion his prey?
    Or satisfy the desire of the young lions,
40. When they couch in their dens,
    And lie in wait in the thicket?
41. Who provideth for the raven his food,
    When his young cry unto God,
    When they are worn down for lack of food?

---

gence to the meteors of the air?" Schultens and Rosenmüller explain it of the various phenomena that appear in the sky—as lightning, thunder, meteoric lights, etc.

37.—*Pour out.*—So Umbreit and Wolfsohn, from an Arabic signification of the word.

39.—Another chapter ought to have begun here, as there is a transition to a new subject.

40.—*When they couch.*—For the purpose of springing upon their prey.—*Lie in wait.*—The usual posture of the lion when he seeks his prey. He places himself in some unobserved position in a dense thicket, or crouches upon the ground so as not to be seen, and then springs suddenly upon his victim.

41.—*Who provideth for the raven.*—Scheutzer *(in loc.)* suggests, that the reason why the *raven* is specified here rather than other fowls is, that it is an offensive bird, and that God means to state that no object, however regarded by man, is beneath *His* notice. He provides for the wants of *all* His creatures.—*When his young.*—There are various opinions expressed in regard to this subject by the Rabbinical writers, and by the ancients generally. Some say, that "when the old ravens see the young coming into the world which are not black, they regard them as the offspring of serpents, and flee away from them, and God takes care of them." Rabbi Solomon says that in this condition they are nourished by the flies and worms that are generated in their nests; and the same opinion was held by the Arabian writers, Haritius, Alkuazin, and Damir. Pliny (lib. x., c. 12) says, that the old ravens expel the strongest of their young from the nest, and compel them to fly. This is the time, when the young ravens are represented as calling upon God for food. See Scheutzer, Physica Sacra, *in loc.*, and Bochart, Hieroz. P. ii., lib. ii., c. 2.—*Worn down.*—The root is not "taah," *to go astray,* but "latha," *to comminute, to wear away.*

XXXIX 1. Knowest thou the time
When the wild goats of the rock bring forth?
Canst thou observe the birth-throes of the hind?
2. Canst thou number the months they fulfil?
Knowest thou the time when they bring forth,
3. When they contract, and give birth to their young,
And cast forth their girding pains?
4. Their young ones break away;
They thrive in the desert;
They go off, and return no more.——
5. Who hath sent out the wild-ass free?
Or the bands of the wild-mule, who hath loosed,

1.—*Knowest thou.*—The point in the enquiry here is not in regard of the *time* when these animals produced their young, or the period of their gestation, which might probably be known, but in regard to the attention and care which was needful for them when they were so far removed from the observance of man, and had no human aid. —*The wild goats.*—The "Ibex."—Its habitation is on the tops of the highest rocks, where its perpetual leaping from precipice to precipice, together with the kids, exposes them to many perils, that without a singular care of Providence the breed must perish.—Rashi observes: "The wild goat hates her young, and when the time to bring forth is at hand, she goes purposely on the top of the rocks, that her young may fall down and be killed; but God sends an eagle to receive the young in his wings." *The hind.*—The hind is a lovely creature, of an elegant shape, and its hair is of great price. It is noted for its swiftness and the sureness of its step. The rutting-time is at the beginning of autumn. They go eight months, and bring forth in the spring.

3.—*When they contract.*—The sense of "bowing down," "crouching," is here inapposite; the verb means, *they contract*, or *draw their limbs together*, for the sake of acquiring an expulsory power. The difficulty with which these creatures bring forth their young is taken notice of by Pliny, Nat. Hist. Lib. viii. 32, and Rashi *in loc.*

4.—*Break away.*—Parkhurst has given the true idea of this verb. *They break away*, either from the womb (alluding to their vigorous efforts even before they are brought forth) or from their dams almost as soon as dropt, as not needing their further care.

5.—*The wild mule.*—Pallas has described it as distinguished by having solid hoofs; an uniform colour; no cross on the back, and the tail hairy at the tip only. The colour is brownish on the upper part of the body; white beneath, and on the buttocks; with a blackish list along the back. It inhabits Arabia, China, Siberia, and Tartary, in grassy, saline plains, or salt wastes, as mentioned in the ensuing verse: but avoids woods, and snowy mountains; is timid, swift, and untameable; its hearing and smell are acute, neighing more sonorous than that of the horse; in size and habits resembling a mule; but,

6. Whose home I have made the wilderness,
And the barren land his dwelling?
7. He scorneth the uproar of the city;
The cry of the driver he heedeth not;
8. The range of the mountains is his pasture,
And he seeketh after every green thing.——
9. Will the REEM be willing to serve thee?
Will he abide all night at thy crib?
10. Canst thou bind him with a yoke to the plough?
Or will he harrow the valleys after thee?
11. Canst thou trust him because his strength is great?
Or canst thou commit thy labour to him?
12. Canst thou depend on him to bring in thy seed,
And gather thy threshing-floor?——

13. Gavest thou to the careless ostrich its wings,
Or the pinions and feathers to the stork?

though called the wild mule, is not a hybrid production; the ears and tail resemble those of the zebra; the hoofs and body those of the ass; the limbs those of the horse. Its length is five feet. The following comments are agreeable to this description.——

7.—*The cry of the driver.*—The Hebrew word properly means *a collector of taxes*, or *revenue*, and hence an oppressor, and a driver of cattle. The allusion is to a driver; and the meaning is that he is not subject to restraint, but enjoys the most unlimited freedom.

9.—*Reem.*—The Targum and the Syriac retain the Hebrew word. Jerome, Good, Barnes, and others: "Rhinoceros;" Gesenius, Herder, Umbreit, Noyes, and Professor Robinson: "Buffalo;" Rosenmüller, Scott, Hewlett, and others: "Onyx" or wild-bull. I prefer therefore to retain the Hebrew word.

11.—*Because his strength is great.*—Canst thou consider his strength as a reason why important interests might be intrusted to him?—*Commit thy labour.*—The *avails* of thy labour—the harvest.

12.—*Thy seed.*—If the sheaves of the harvest were laid on him, there would be no certainty that he would convey them where the farmer wished them.

13.—All commentators have despaired of making any sense out of the Hebrew in this verse, and there have been almost as many conjectures as there have been expositors. Schultens renders:
"The wing of the ostrich is exulting:
But is it the wing and the plumage of the stork?"
Rosenmüller:
"The wing of the ostrich exults!
Truly its wing and plumage is like that of the stork!"

14. She leaveth her eggs on the ground,
   And warmeth them in the sand;
15. And forgetteth that the foot may crush them,
   Or that the wild beast may break them.
16. To her young she is cruel, as if they were not hers;
   Unconcerned if her labour be in vain;

Good :
 "The wing of the ostrich-tribe is for flapping,
 But of the stork and the falcon for flight."
Herder:
 "A wing with joyous cry is uplifted yonder;
 Is it the wing and feather of the ostrich?"
Professor Lee :
 "Wilt thou confide in the exulting of the wings of the ostrich?
 Or in her choice feathers and head plumage,
 When she leaveth her eggs in the earth?"——
Barnes:
 "A wing of exulting fowls moves joyfully!
 Is it the wing and the plumage of the stork?"
I have followed Wolfsohn.—From the following verses it would appear that the ostrich is indeed *careless*.

14.—*Leaveth her eggs on the ground.*—The ostrich builds her nest on some sandy hillock, in the most barren and solitary recesses of the desert. She sits upon her eggs, as other birds do; but then she so often wanders, and so far, in search of food, that frequently the eggs are rotten in consequence of her long absence from them. The ostrich, Dr. Shaw remarks, lays usually from thirty to fifty eggs; they are very large, some of them being above five inches in diameter, and weighing fifteen pounds.

15.—*And forgetteth.*—Damir, an Arabic writer says : "When the ostrich goes forth from her nest, if she finds the egg of another ostrich, she sits on that, and forgets her own; and when driven away by hunters, she never returns." Ottomanus says : "Every animal loves its own progeny except the ostrich."

16.—*She is cruel.*—The ostrich is destitute of natural affection for her young. This sentiment occurs in Lam. iv., v. 3. "The daughter of my people is become cruel, like the ostriches in the wilderness." This opinion is controverted by Buffon; but is sustained by those who have most attentively observed the habits of the ostrich. Dr. Shaw says : "On the least noise or trivial occasion, she forsakes her eggs, or her young ones, to which perhaps she never returns; or if she does, it may be too late either to restore life to the one, or to preserve the lives of the others." Paxton says: "The Arabs meet sometimes with whole nests of these eggs undisturbed, some of which are sweet and good, and others addled and corrupted; others again have their young ones of different growths, according to the time it may be presumed they have been forsaken by the dam. They oftener meet a few of the little ones, not bigger than well-grown pullets, half-starved, straggling and moaning about like so many distressed orphans for their mothers."

17. For God hath withheld wisdom from her,
   And hath not imparted to her understanding;
18. Yet, when she urgeth herself forward,
   She laugheth at the horse and his rider.——

19. Hast thou given to the horse his strength?
   Hast thou clothed his neck with a quivering mane?
20. Canst thou make him leap as the locust?
   How terrible the strength of his snorting!
21. He paweth in the valley; He exalteth in his strength;
   He rusheth on to meet the clashing host;
22. He laugheth at fear, nor is he terrified;
   He turneth not back at the sight of the sword;
23. Against him rattleth the quiver in vain;
   The glittering spear, and the lance;

18.—*Urgeih herself forward.*—To escape her pursuer.—*She laugheth.*—She runs faster than the fleetest horse, and easily escapes. The strength and swiftness of the ostrich Adamson hath well described: He was in possession of two tame ostriches, and "to try their strength" says he, "I made a full-grown negro mount the smallest, and two others the largest. This burden did not seem to me at all disproportioned to their strength. At first, they went a pretty high trot, and when they were heated a little, they *expanded their wings* as if they were *to catch the wind,* and they moved with such fleetness as to seem to be off the ground." I have also to observe that the verses 13-18 are not in their proper place. They should come after verse 25 or after verse 30.

19.—*The horse.*—The war-horse is here intended —*Quivering mane.*—Auth. Version : "Clothed his neck with thunder;" but there seems to be something incongruous in the idea of making *thunder* the *clothing* of the neck of the horse. Herder: "And clothed its neck with its flowing mane." Good : "With the thunder-flash." Prof. Lee: "With scorn." Barnes : "With thunder." Umbreit : "With loftiness." Sept. : "With terror." Schultens : "With rapid quivering."

20.—*Leap.*—This agility expresseth his joy to find himself in the rank of battle.

22-23.—These verses are out of their place ; they ought to come after verse 25. His courage and daring spirit, is plainly the finishing-stroke in the description.

23.—*The quiver.*—The quiver was a case made for containing arrows. It was slung over the shoulder, so that it could be easily reached to draw out an arrow. The rattling of the quiver was caused by the fact that the arrows were thrown somewhat loosely into the case or the quiver, and that in the rapid motion of the warrior they were shaken against each other.

24. In fierceness and rage he swalloweth the ground;
   Nor can he be restrained at the sound of the trumpet;
25. When the trumpet soundeth, he saith: "Aha!"
   And from afar he smelleth the battle——
   The war-cry of the chiefs, and the shouting.——

26. Doth the hawk fly by thy wisdom,
   And spread his wings toward the south?
27. Doth the eagle mount aloft at thy command,
   And make his nest on high?
28. On the rock he dwelleth, and abideth
   Upon the craggy rock, in a secure place;
29. Thence he watcheth for prey;
   For his eyes behold afar off;
30. His young ones suck up blood;
   And where the slain are, there is he.——

24.—*Swalloweth the ground.*—He runs swiftly over it.

25.—*He saith "Aha."*—The reference is to the impatient neighing of the war-horse about to rush into the conflict.

26.—*The hawk.*—Most of the species of hawks, we are told, are birds of passage. The hawk therefore is produced as a specimen of that astonishing instinct, which teaches them to know when to migrate out of one country into another for the benefit of food, or a warmer climate.—See Jerem. viii., v. 7.

27-30.—How descriptive are these verses! From the highest promontories, and his loftiest flights, he discerns his prey on the ground. He pounces on his prey, and bears it alive to his nest almost in the same instant. The eagle is fond of flesh, and sucks the blood, with both which he nourishes his young.

28.—In Damir it is said that the blind poet Besar, son of Jazidi, being asked, if God would give him the choice to be an animal, what he would be, said that he would wish to be nothing else than an *alokab*, a species of the eagle, for they dwelt in places in which no wild animal could have access.—Scheutzer, *Phy. Sac.*, *in loc.*

29.—"Of all animals, the eagle has the quickest eye; but his sense of smelling is far inferior to that of the vulture. He never pursues, therefore, but in sight."—GOLDSMITH.

30.—*Suck up blood.*—The principal food of the *young* eagle is blood. See Scheutzer, *Phy. Sac.*, *in loc.*—Anderson, in his History of Iceland, asserts that in that island children of four and five years of age have been carried off by an eagle.

CHAPTER XL.

1. Moreover, the Lord answered Job, and said:
2. Is he that contended with the Almighty now instructed?
   He that reproved God is he ready to answer?
3. Then Job answered the Lord, and said:
4. Behold I am vile, what shall I answer Thee?
   I will lay my hand upon my mouth.
5. Once did I speak, but I will speak no more—
   A second time I will not do it.
6. Then the Lord answered Job out of the whirlwind, and said:
7. Gird up thy loins like a man;
   I will ask of thee, and do thou inform Me!
8. Wilt thou reverse My judgment?
   Wilt thou condemn Me, that thou mayest be just?
9. Hast thou an arm like God?
   Or canst thou thunder with a voice like Him?
10. Adorn thyself then with grandeur and majesty,
    And array thyself with splendour and glory;

1.—*Answered Job.*—The word *answered* is used here, as it is often, in the Scriptures, to continue an argument.

2.— God had paused, after the sublime exhibition of His Majesty and power in the previous chapters, to give him an opportunity, as he wished, to carry his cause before Him. The result is stated in verse 3-4.—Job had now nothing to say.—*Is he ready to answer.*—Not as the Auth. Vers. would seem to imply, that he who reproves God must be held responsible for it, but that Job, who had expressed the wish to carry his cause before God, had now an opportunity to do so.

5.—I have followed Wolfsohn.—This rendering is in accordance with the ancient versions and several Hebrew MSS.

6.—God resumes the argument which had been interrupted, in order to give Job an opportunity to speak.

7.—*Gird up thy loins.*—Put forth all thy strength, and explain to me what will now be said.

8.— *Wilt thou reverse.*—Job had complained of the dealings of God, and this was the same as saying, that he could show that those dealings should have been different from what they were.

9.—*An arm.*—The arm is the symbol of strength. The question here is whether he would venture to compare his strength with the omnipotence of God.—*Thunder.*—Thunder is a symbol of the majesty of the Most High.

11. Let loose the fury of thy wrath;
    Look on every one that is proud, and abase him;
12. Look on every one that is proud, and humble him;
    Yea, tread down the wicked in their place;
13. Hide them in the dust together;
    In secret places bind up their faces:
14. Then will I also give thee praise;
    For thine own right hand can save thee.——
15. Behold now the hippopotamus,
    Which I made as well as thyself;
    He feedeth on grass like the horse;
16. Behold now his strength is in his loins;
    And his vigour in the muscles of his belly;
17. When he lusteth his tail is like a cedar;
    The sinews of his testicles are twisted together;
18. His bones are like strong pieces of copper;
    His back-bone like a bar of iron;

11.—*Let loose*—Root "patzah," not "naphatz," as the Auth. version.

12.—*In their place.*—In the very place where they are, crush them to the dust.—It is implied that God was able to do this, and He appeals to it as a proof of His power.

13.—*In secret places.*—This may refer to a dungeon or prison. The idea is that God had power to restrain and control the haughty and the wicked, and He appeals to Job to do the same.

15.—*The Hippopotamus.*—Bochart maintained, and since his time the opinion has been generally acquiesced in, that the *Hippopotamus* of the Nile was referred to.—See also the "Measseph," 5549.—*He feedeth on grass.*—This is mentioned as a remarkable property of this animal.—For it might have been supposed that an animal so huge and fierce, and armed with such a set of teeth, would be carnivorous, like the lion or the tiger.—It is also remarkable that an animal that commonly lived in the water should be graminivorous, as if it were wholly a land animal.—The common food of the *Hippopotamus* is *fish*. But it often happens that this kind of food is not found in sufficient abundance, and the animal is then forced on land, where it commits great depredations among plantations of sugar-cane and grain. See Sparrman, *Travels through South Africa*, p. 563. (German edition.)

16.—*In his loins.*—This proves that the *elephant* cannot be referred to; for *his* strength is in the neck, whilst the principal power of the hippopotamus is in the loins.

17.—What the *object* of this description is I do not know.

19. He is chief among the works of God;
 He that made him furnished him with a sword;
20. Surely the mountains bring him forth food;
 Where all the beasts of the field play about.
21. He lieth under the lotus-trees;
 In the covert of the reeds and marshy places;
22. The lotus-trees cover him with their shade;
 The willows of the river surround him;
23. Lo, the stream overfloweth and he hasteneth not away;
 He is unmoved though the Jordan rush to his mouth.
24. Who can take him openly?
 Or draw a cord through his nose?——

25. Canst thou draw out the crocodile with a hook?
 Or fasten his tongue with a cord?

18.—The circumstance here adverted to is remarkable because the common residence of the animal is the water, and the bones of aquatic animals are generally hollow, and much less firm than those of land animals.

19.—*With a sword.*—The allusion is to his strong sharp teeth, bearing a resemblance to a sword, and designed either for defence, or for the purpose of cutting the long grass on which he feeds when on the land.

20.—*The mountains.*—Though he is in the water a considerable portion of his time, yet he also wanders to the mountains, and finds his food there.—*Play about.*—It is remarkable that an animal so large and mighty, and armed with such a set of teeth, should not be carnivorous.—The truth is however, that the characteristics here given to "Behemoth," will not *strictly* apply either to the *hippopotamus* or the *elephant.*—See Rosenmüller's elaborate Scholium on verse 15.

21.—*Lotus-trees.*—So Schultens, Wolfsohn, Gesenius, Lee, and others. Vulg., Syr., Aben Ezra, Rashi, and Rosenmüller: "shady trees."—*Marshy places.*—There the *elephant* is never found.

23.—*The stream overfloweth.*—He lives in the water as well as on the land, and is unmoved even though the impetuous torrent of a swollen river should overwhelm him.—*Rush to his mouth.*—Though the whole river Jordan should seem to pour down upon him, as if it were about to rush into his mouth, it would not disturb him. The Jordan is here mentioned, *not* that the hippopotamus is an inhabitant of the Jordan, but as put for any deep and violent river; for such the Jordan is in the time of its overflowing.

25.—The Polyglot and most versions begin the xli. ch. at this verse. This division is preferable to that of the Hebrew.—*The crocodile.*—Hasselquist observes, that this ferocious animal far from being "drawn up by a hook," bites off and destroys all fishing-tackle

26. Canst thou put a hook into his nose?
   Or pierce his jaw with a ring?
27. Will he make many supplications unto thee?
   Will he speak soft words unto thee?
28. Will he make a covenant with thee,
   That thou mayest take him for a perpetual servant?
29. Canst thou play with him as with a bird?
   Or canst thou bind him for thy maidens?
30. Will friends feast over him?
   Will they divide him among the merchants?
31. Canst thou fill his skin with barbed irons?
   Or his head with fish spears?——

* * * * * * *

32. Lay now thy hand on him!
   Remember! thou wilt not renew the conflict!
33. Behold! the hope of taking him is vain!
   Doth he not faint even at the sight of him?

---

of this kind, which is thrown out in the river. "I found," says he, "in one that I opened, *two hooks*, which it had swallowed, one sticking in the stomach, and the other in a part of the thick membrane which covers the palate." *Travels*, page 440.

26.—*Pierce his jaws.*—Mr. Bruce, speaking of the manner of fishing in the Nile, says that when a fisherman has caught a fish, he draws it to the shore, and puts a strong iron ring into its jaw; to this ring is fastened a rope by which the fish is attached to the shore, which he then throws again into the water.

27.—*Will he make many supplications.*—Will he quietly submit to you.—*Speak soft words.*—Pleading for his life in tones of tender and plaintive supplication.

29.—*Bind him for thy maidens.*—For their amusement.—For such purposes, doubtless, birds were caught and caged.

30.—Translators greatly differ, and it is not easy to determine the true sense.—*Merchants.*—Hebrew, "Canaanites."—The Phœnicians of Zidon are probably meant.

31.—*Barbed irons.*—*Fish-spears.*—The impenetrability of the skin is here intimated.

I have here to remark that verses 32-33 of ch. xl., and 1-2 of ch. xli., (or, according to Auth. Vers., verses 8-11 of ch. xli.,) are torn from their proper connection. They should follow verse 25, ch. xli. (*i.e.* verse 34 in the Auth. Version.)

32.—*Lay now thy hand.*—Endeavour to seize him.—*Will not renew.*—The conflict would be fatal to thee.

33.—This is spoken to Job.—This change from the *second* to the *third* person occurs frequently in the Scriptures, especially in this Book.

XLI.
1. He hath not the courage to arouse him!..........
   And who was it then that stood insolently before Me?
2. Who hath done Me a favour that I must repay him?
   All that is under the heaven is Mine!

* * * * * * * *

3. I will not be silent concerning his limbs,
   His power, and the fitness of his armature.
4. Who can uncover his mailed face?
   Who can approach the doubling of his jaws?
5. The doors of his face who can open?
   The rows of his teeth are terrible;—
6. His back is like strong shields;
   Closed together as with a seal;
7. They are joined one to another,
   So that no air cometh between them;

1.—God says to Job: "If one of My *creatures* is so formidable that thou darest not attack him, how then couldst thou have the impudence, as it was thy wish, to contend with Me?"

2.—*Done me a favour.*—Compare Micah vi., v. 6.—*All that is.*—Man ought therefore to submit to me without a murmur, and to receive with gratitude what I choose to confer.

3.—*I will not be silent.*—This is the commencement of a more particular description of the crocodile, and ought to have followed after verse 31 of ch. xl.—*And the fitness.*—There is no *beauty* in an animal like the one here described, yet there is a *grace* or fitness in its means of defence, which could not fail to attract admiration. So Gesenius, Umbreit, and Noyes.

4.—*His mailed face.*—So Schultens.—*The doubling of his jaws.*—Who dare approach a double row of teeth so formidable? Schultens and Prof. Lee, however, suppose it means that no one can come near to him and *double the bit* upon him, *i.e.*, cast the bit or noose over his nose, so as to secure him by doubling it, or passing it around him.

5.—*The doors of his face.*—His mouth.—No one would dare to open his mouth.—*The rows of his teeth.*—Bochart says that it has sixty teeth, and those much larger than in proportion to the size of the body. Some of them, he says, stand out; some of them are serrated, or like a saw, fitting into each other when the mouth is closed, and some come together in the manner of a comb, so that the grasp of the animal is very tenacious and fearful.

6.—*Strong shields.*—His back is covered with scales that resemble the strong plates of shields.

8. They cleave fast to each other;
   They stick together, and cannot be separated.
9. When he sneezeth, the light sparkleth;
   And his eyes are like the eyelids of the morning.
10. Out of his mouth go firebrands;
    Sparks of fire burst forth;
11. From his nostrils issueth smoke,
    As from a boiling pot or caldron;
12. His breath kindleth coals,
    And a flame issueth from his mouth;
13. Strength abideth upon his neck!
    Destruction danceth before him;
14. The flakes of his flesh are closed together;
    They are firm upon him, they cannot be moved;

8.—*They cleave fast.*—It is this which makes the crocodile so difficult to be killed.

9.—*The light sparkleth.*—Such is the violence and heat of the air that is repelled from his nose when he sneezes, that it sparkles in the sunbeams.—*His eyes.*—The eyes of the crocodile are small, but they are so remarkable, that when the Egyptians would represent *the morning* by an hieroglyphic, they painted a crocodile's eye.

10.—*Out of his mouth.*—Here the creature is described in pursuit of its prey on the land.—His mouth is then open, his blood inflamed, his breath is thrown out with prodigious vehemence, it appears like volumes of smoke, and is heated to that degree, as to seem a flaming fire.

11.—Bertram, in his *Travels in North and South Carolina*, p. 116, says: "While I was seeking a place of rest, I encountered an alligator, that in the neighbouring lake rushed through the canes that grew on its banks. He inflated his enormous body, and swung his tail high in the air; a thick smoke streamed from his wide open nostrils, with a sound that made the earth tremble."— Rosenmüller, *Alte und Neue Morgenland*, No. 778.

12.—A similar phrase is found in a sublime description of the anger of the Almighty, in Psalm xviii. v. 8:
   "There went up a smoke out of his nostrils,
   And fire out of his mouth devoured:
   Coals were kindled by it."

13.—*Strength and destruction* are here represented as animated beings. The former is seated on the neck of the crocodile, to signify the extraordinary inflexibility of that part. The other leaps and dances before him, when he pursues his prey, to express the terrible slaughter which he makes.

14.—*The flakes.*—The idea is that his flesh and inward parts are remarkably compact and tough.

15. His heart is as firm as a stone;
    Yea, firm as the nether-millstone;
16. When he riseth up, the mighty are afraid;
    They lose themselves at the tumult of the sea;
17. Should the sword reach him it will not adhere;
    Nor will the spear, the dart, or the javelin;
18. He regardeth iron as straw,
    And copper as rotten wood;
19. The arrow will not put him to flight;
    Sling-stones are turned back as stubble;
20. Clubs are regarded by him as stubble;
    He laugheth at the brandishing of the spear;
21. Under him are the weapons of the artificer;
    He spreadeth pointed darts on the mud;
22. He maketh the deep to boil like a pot;
    The sea he maketh thick as ointment;
23. After him he leaves a shining path;
    One would think the deep to be hoary;
24. Upon earth there is not his like;
    He is made free from fear;
25. He looketh disdainfully upon all that is lofty;
    He is king over all the sons of pride.*

15.—*Nether-millstone.*—Why the *lower* stone was the hardest, is not quite apparent. Perhaps a more solid stone might have been chosen for this, because it was supposed that there was more wear on the *lower* than the *upper* stone.

16.—*The mighty.*—Even the mightiest acquatic animals

17.—*Should the sword.*—The usual instruments of attack, make no impression on him.

19.—*Turned back.*—They produce no more effect on him than it would to throw stubble at him.

21.—*Under him.*—He reduceth under him.

22.—*Ointment.*—Bochart supposes that there is an allusion here to the smell of musk, which it is said the crocodile has, and by which the waters through which he passes seem to be perfumed.

25.—*He looketh disdainfully.*—See Aben Ezra and Rashi on Solomon's songs, ch. i., v. 6.

*Here ought now to follow ch. xl., vv. 32-33, and ch. xli., vv. 1-2; for with these verses ends this sublime address of the Almighty.

CHAPTER XLII.

1. Then Job answered the Lord, and said:
2. I know that Thou canst do everything,
   And that no purpose of Thine can be hindered.
3. [Thou askedst]
   "Who is he that darkeneth counsel without knowledge?"
   I have indeed uttered what I understood not;
   Things too wonderful for me, which I knew not,
4. [When I said:] "Hear now and I will speak,
   I will ask Thee, and do Thou teach me."
5. I have heard of Thee by the hearing of the ear;
   But now mine eye seeth Thee;
6. Wherefore I abhor myself,
   And repent in dust and ashes.

7. And it came to pass after the Lord had spoken these words to Job, that the Lord said to Eliphaz, the Temanite: "My wrath is kindled against thee, and "thy two friends; for ye have not spoken concerning
8. "Me as hath my servant Job: Therefore take for "yourselves seven bullocks and seven rams, and go

---

2.—*I know.*—This is an acknowledgment that God was omnipotent, and that man ought to be submissive under the putting forth of His infinite power.

3.—*I have indeed uttered.*—This is the language of true humility and penitence, and shows that Job had at heart a profound veneration for God, however much he had been led away by the severity of his sufferings to make use of improper expressions.

4.—In this verse Job designs to make confession of the impropriety of his language on former occasions, in the presumptuous and irreverent manner in which he had demanded a trial of argument with God.

5.—*By the hearing of the ear.*—His views of God before were dark and obscure.—*But now.*—His apprehensions of God were clear and bright as if he actually *saw* God.

6.—*I abhor myself.*—I see that I am a sinner to be loathed and abhorred.

7.—*To Eliphaz.*—Eliphaz had been uniformly first in the argument with Job, and hence he is particularly addressed here. He seems to have been the most aged and respectable of the three friends, and in fact the speeches of the others are often a mere echo of his.

"to my servant Job, and offer for yourselves a burnt-
"offering; but my servant Job must pray for you—
"for his person I will accept—lest I deal with you
"after your folly; for ye have not spoken so concern-
"ing Me, as hath my servant Job."

9. Then Eliphaz, the Temanite; and Bildad, the Shuhite; and Zophar, the Naamathite, went and did as the Lord had commanded them; and the Lord accepted the person of Job.
10. And the Lord restored to Job his loss, after he had prayed for his friends; yea, the Lord gave to Job
11. twice as much as he had before. Then came to him all his brethren, and all his sisters, and all his former acquaintances, and ate bread with him in his house; and condoled with him, and comforted him over all the evil that the Lord had brought upon him; and every one gave him a KESITAH, and every one a ring of gold.
12. Thus the Lord blessed the latter days of Job more than his beginning; for he had fourteen thousand sheep, six thousand camels, a thousand yoke of oxen,
13. and a thousand she-asses; He also had seven sons
14. and three daughters; and he called the name of the first Jemima, of the second Kezia, and of the third
15. Keren-happuch. And in all the land were no women found so beautiful as the daughters of Job; and their father gave them an inheritance among their brethren.
16. And Job lived after this a hundred and forty years, and saw his sons, and his sons' sons, four generations.
17. Then Job died, old and full of days.

8.—*Seven.*—The number *seven* was a common number in offering animals for sacrifice. See Lev. xxiii., v. 18; Numb. xxix., v. 32.— *After your folly.*—As their folly had deserved.

9.—*Accepted.*—God accepted his prayers on behalf of his friends.

11.—*Brethren—Sisters.*—See ch. xix., v. 17, and note.—*Kesitah.*— A coin.—This word occurs only here and in Gen. xxxii., v. 19.

LIST OF SUBSCRIBERS.

	COPIES.
Belfast.	
Jaffe, M., Esq.	1
Birmingham.	
Blankensee, M., Esq. ..	1
Davis, J., Esq. ..	1
Emanuel, J., Esq. ..	1
Hillner, S., Esq. ..	1
Joseph, J., Esq. ..	1
Joseph, M., Esq. ..	1
Lazarus, J., Esq. ..	1
Meyers, —., Esq. ..	1
Monaet, J., Esq. ..	1
Nathan, H., Esq. ..	1
Phillips, P., Esq. ..	1
Rothschild, J., Esq. ..	1
Solomon, J., Esq. ..	1
White, W., Esq. ..	1
Bradford.	
Brear, Th., Esq. ..	1
Cohn, J. E., Esq. ..	2
Drake, J., Esq. ..	2
Semon, Charles, Esq. ..	2
Brighton	
Jacobs, A. C., Rev. ..	1
Nuremberg, M. S., Rev. ..	1
Bristol.	
Benjamin, J., Rev. ..	1
Berliner, B., Rev. ..	1
Mosely, A., Esq. ..	1
Cheltenham.	
Phillips, R., Rev. ..	1
Coventry.	
Friedlander, A. E., Esq. ..	1
Dawlish.	
Solomon, Leon, Esq. ..	5

	COPIES.
Durham.	
Fowler, J. J., Rev. ..	1
Hartlepools, The	
Benjamin, S., Esq. ..	1
Cassel, A., Esq. ..	1
Levy, J., Esq. ..	1
Lotinga, C., Esq. ..	1
Mosesson, J., Rev. ..	1
Tristram, H. B., Rev. Dr. ..	1
Hull.	
Alper, S., Esq. ..	1
Cohen, S., Esq. ..	1
Sampson, S. A., Esq. ..	1
Leeds.	
Bachner, F., Esq. ..	1
Bernstein, M., Esq. ..	1
Blasebalk, N., Esq. ..	1
Blashker, S., Esq. ..	1
Bolland, J., Esq. ..	1
Camrass, S., Esq. ..	1
Cohen, M., Esq. ..	1
Danziger, E., Rev. ..	2
Davis, Edw., Esq. ..	2
Goodman, L., Esq. ..	1
Goodman, M., Esq. ..	1
Gross, J., Esq. ..	1
Grunthal, A., Esq. ..	1
Grunthal, J., Esq. ..	1
Israel, J., Esq. ..	2
Ludzki, R., Esq. ..	1
Scattergood, Th., Dr. ..	1
Tanenberg, M., Esq. ..	1
Liverpool.	
Barnett, P., Esq. ..	1
Lazarus, J., Esq. ..	1
Lublin, E., Esq. ..	1
Robinson, R., Esq. ..	2
Yates, E. W., Esq. ..	2

LIST OF SUBSCRIBERS.—*(Continued.)*

London.

	COPIES.
Adler, N. M., Rev. Dr.	1
Beddington, H. L., Esq.	10
Benjamin, M. H., Esq.	3
Bergtheil, J., Esq.	1
Castello, M., Esq.	2
Cohen, Aaron, Esq.	2
Cohen, David, Esq.	4
Cohen, M. X., Esq.	3
Emanuel, L., Esq.	1
Goldsmid, Julian, Esq., M.P.	2
Guedalla, H., Esq.	3
Henriques, J. Q., Esq.	1
Jessel, G., Sir, Esq., M.P. *(Solicitor General)*	2
Joseph, N. S., Esq.	1
Keeling, H. L., Esq.	2
Lazarus, L., Esq.	2
Levison, J. L., Dr.	1
Meyers, Victor M., Esq.	1
Miers, S. L., Esq.	1
Mocatta, F. D., Esq.	4
Montefiore, Nath., Esq.	2
Nathan, L., Esq.	5
Rothschild, L. de, Baron, Esq., M.P.	25
Rothschild, L. M., Esq.	3
Sassoon, R. D., Esq.	5
Spiers, B., Rev.	1
Vallentine, P., Esq.	6
Worms, H. de, Baron, Esq.	4

Manchester.

	COPIES.
Gottheil, Rev. Dr.	1
Landstein, P., Esq.	1

Newcastle-on-Tyne.

Cohen, E., Rev.	1
Cohen, F., Esq.	1
Harris, S. H., Rev.	1
Jacobs, J., Esq.	1

Nottingham.

Samuel, J., Esq.	1

Paris.

Alliance, Isr., Universelle.	5
Cohn, Albert, Dr.	2

Sheffield.

Guttman, T. Mrs.	1
Levi, S., Esq.,	1
Marks, A., Mrs.	1
Moss, J. Mrs.	1

Southampton.

Alexander, S., Rev.	1
Emanuel, S. M. Esq., J.P.	1

Wolverhampton.

Gordon, S., Esq.	1

www.ingramcontent.com/pod-product-compliance
Lightning Source LLC
Chambersburg PA
CBHW022129160426
43197CB00009B/1204